Wood Pellet Smoker and Grill Cookbook

200 Delicious Recipes to Master the Barbeque and Enjoy it with Friends and Family

PETER DEVON

Contents

Introduction

The clinical definition of a wood pellet smoker-grill is a barbecue pit that uses compressed hardwood sawdust like apple, cherry, hickory, maple, mesquite, oak, and other wood pellets to smoke, grill, roast, and bake. The wood pellet smoker grill provides you with flavor profiles and moisture that only hardwood cooking can achieve. Depending on the manufacturer and model, grill temperatures range from 150°F to well over 600°F on many models. The days when people say you can't sear and grill on a wood pellet smoker-grill are gone! Wood pellet smoker-grills provide succulence, convenience, and safety unmatched by charcoal or gas grills. The smoke profile is milder than other smokers you might be used to. Because of their design, they produce the versatility and benefits of a convection oven. Wood pellet smoker-grills are safe and simple to operate.

The basic components of a wood pellet smoker-grill are:

HOPPER—The hopper is where the wood pellets are stored. Ensure that you maintain an ample number of pellets depending on the length of the cook, the temperature of the cook, and the hopper capacity.

AUGER—The pellets are then fed through the auger, the feed mechanism that delivers the pellets to the firepot.

FIREPOT—This is where the wood pellets that heat the grill are ignited and burn. The large hole in the firepot is for the pellet tube, which houses the auger; the lower center hole below it is for the igniter rod, and the other holes are for the fan airflow. It's a good practice to empty or vacuum out the ashes after every few cooks in order to allow the igniter to work more efficiently.

IGNITER ELEMENT/ROD—This rod ignites the wood pellets in the firepot. With the firepot removed you can see the igniter rod and the pellet feed tube that the auger uses to deliver pellets to the firepot.

FAN—The fan is very important as it maintains a variable and/or constant flow of air, keeping the pellets

HEAT DEFLECTOR—The heat deflector is a specially designed plate that covers the firepot. Its purpose is to absorb the heat and spread it out evenly below the grease/drip pan, effectively turning your wood pellet smoker-grill into a wood-fired convection oven. burning in the firepot and resulting in convection cooking.

GREASE/DRIP PAN—The grease pan is used for indirect cooking, smoking, roasting, and baking. It routes the grease produced during cooking to the grease bucket. Scrape off any caked-on residue from cooks as required. If using foil (highly recommended), replace the foil every few cooks.

FLAME ZONE PAN—For direct grilling at high temperatures. Used in conjunction with searing grates and griddle accessories.

GREASE BUCKET—The grease bucket collects runoff grease and fat from cooking sessions. Grease accumulation depends on how much you choose to trim fat caps and excess fat from meat and poultry. Lining your grease bucket with foil helps with cleanups. I like to use an old coffee can to store my runoff grease. It's safe to dispose full coffee cans in your garbage.

1.2 Why a Wood Pellet Smoker-Grill?
When looking for your next outdoor cooking device for your barbecue needs, your best option on the market today is a wood pellet smoker-grill. You've used the rest, now use the best! No more buying a new grill every few seasons or needing more than one grill. Wood pellet smoker-grills, allow you to smoke, cook low and slow, roast, bake, and grill, and like propane grills, they preheat in 10 to 15 minutes. With its indirect heat design there are no flare-ups, and you'll never have any of the harsh smoke flavors sometimes generated by charcoal or straight wood fires. A wood pellet smoker-grill not only produces the best moist foods you'll ever experience, but it is by far one of the easiest to operate and maintain. Everything is automated. Merely ensure that your hopper is full of wood pellets and that your unit is plugged into a power source. The only movable parts in a wood pellet smoker-grill are the auger and fan. The tricky part to other types of smoker-grills has always been the necessary monitoring of the units to keep the temperatures steady. This is not necessary with wood pellet smoker-grills because they are designed to maintain temperatures within set guidelines.

1.3 Temperature Control
It's all about control. To quote Ron Popeil on his Ronco rotisserie, "Set it, and forget it!" As we learned earlier, the controller adjusts the rate of pellet flow and the fan to maintain your set-point temperature. For the most part, most manufacturers choose a third-party controller or design their own. Obviously, not all controllers are created equal. Some are just better than others and should be a strong consideration when selecting your wood pellet smoker-grill. Look for a controller that provides pinpoint heat control. Basically, there are three types of controllers: analog, digital, and PID. Analog controllers are the most basic unit. They only provide three positions, known as LMH for low, medium, and high smoke. These controllers are mostly found on entry-level units. They typically do not have an RTD or thermocouple temperature probe to provide a feedback loop. This is the least desirable controller, and I would not recommend a unit with one of these. The temperature on these units wildly fluctuates and is unable to correct itself

for ambient temperatures. The auger on and off durations for low, medium, and high is the only control you have and is usually set by the grill manufacturer.

Digital controllers use an RTD temperature probe to provide a feedback loop. Most digital controllers have a 25-degree Fahrenheit increment setting. With the installation of an RTD temperature probe, some digital controllers are a direct replacement for LMH controllers. Similar to the thermostat in your home, once you reach your preset temperature; the controller runs the auger for a certain number of seconds and then shuts off for a certain number of seconds and goes into an idle mode until the temperature deviates a preset amount. At that time the cycle is repeated. Some digital controllers allow you to adjust the idle mode to compensate for ambient temperatures.

1.4 History of Wood Pellet Smoker-Grills

Today there is a multitude of wood pellet smoker-grill manufacturers providing a wide range of excellent barbecue pits. These units cover a broad spectrum, from entry level to sophisticated pits priced from $300 to over $2,500. Just a few decades ago, this was not the case. Wood pellet smoker-grills were first introduced in the 1990s by a small company in Oregon called Traeger Grills. Years ago, I remember watching Traeger commercials featuring Terry Bradshaw, and ogling Traeger grills at my local Ace Hardware store. Those commercials made it look so simply, and I can now attest to the fact that they were right! The industry only grew by leaps and bounds once Traeger's original patent expired. More and more people became exposed to the fabulous, mouth-watering food from a wood pellet smoker-grill, but as recently as 2008 only two companies manufactured wood pellet smoker-grills: Traeger and its rival MAK, also based in Oregon. Today there are more than 20 brands of excellent wood pellet smoker-grill manufacturers carried by a wide range of outlets from local barbecue stores, butcher shops, feed stores, hardware stores, big box stores, online outlets, and direct from the manufacturer.

Chapter 2: Appetizers and Sides

2.1 Atomic Buffalo Turds
Ingredients:

- 10 medium jalapeño peppers
- 8 ounces regular cream cheese at room temperature ¾ cup shredded Monterey Jack and cheddar
- cheese blend (optional) 1 teaspoon smoked paprika
- 1 teaspoon garlic powder
- ½ teaspoon cayenne pepper
- ½ teaspoon red pepper flakes (optional)
- 20 Little Smokies sausages
- 10 thinly sliced bacon strips, cut in half

Instructions:

- Put your food service gloves on, if using. Wash and slice the jalapeño peppers lengthwise. Using a spoon or paring knife, carefully remove the seeds and veins and discard them. Place the jalapeños on a vegetable grilling tray and set aside.
- In a small bowl, mix the cream cheese, shredded cheese, if using, paprika, garlic powder, cayenne pepper, and red pepper flakes, if using, until fully incorporated.
- Fill the hollowed jalapeño pepper halves with the cream cheese mixture. Wrap half a slice of thin bacon around each jalapeño pepper half.
- Use a toothpick to secure the bacon to the sausage, making sure not to pierce the pepper. Place the ABTs on a grilling tray or pan.
- Configure your wood pellet smoker-grill for indirect cooking and preheat to 250°F using hickory pellets or a blend.
- Smoke the jalapeño peppers at 250°F for approximately 1½ to 2 hours, until the bacon is cooked and crispy.

2.2 Smashed Potato Casserole
Ingredients:

- 8 to 10 bacon slices
- ¼ cup (½ stick) salted butter or bacon grease
- 1 small red onion, sliced thinly
- 1 small green bell pepper, sliced thinly
- 1 small red bell pepper, sliced thinly
- 1 small yellow bell pepper, sliced thinly
- 3 cups mashed potatoes
- ¾ cup sour cream
- 1½ teaspoons Texas Barbecue Rub (page 171) 3 cups shredded sharp cheddar cheese, divided
- 4 cups frozen hash brown potatoes

Instructions:

- Cook the bacon in a large skillet over medium heat until crisp, about 5 minutes on each side. Set the bacon aside.
- Transfer the rendered bacon grease to a glass container.
- In the same large skillet, over medium heat, warm the butter or bacon grease and sauté the red onion and bell peppers until al dente. Set aside.
- Spray a 9 × 11-inch casserole dish with nonstick cooking spray, and spread the mashed potatoes in the bottom of the dish.
- Layer the sour cream over the mashed potatoes and season with Texas Barbecue Rub.
- Layer the sautéed vegetables on top of the potatoes, retaining the butter or bacon grease in the pan.
- Sprinkle with 1½ cups of the sharp cheddar cheese followed by the frozen hash brown potatoes.
- Spoon the remaining butter or bacon grease from the sautéed vegetables over the hash browns and top with crumbled bacon.
- Top with the remaining 1½ cups of sharp cheddar cheese and cover the casserole dish with a lid or aluminum foil.
- Configure your wood pellet smoker-grill for indirect cooking and preheat to 350°F using your pellets of choice.
- Bake the smashed potato casserole for 45 to 60 minutes, until the cheese is bubbling.
- Let rest for 10 minutes before serving.

2.3 Bacon-Wrapped Asparagus
Ingredients:

- 1-pound fresh thick asparagus (15 to 20 spears)
- extra-virgin olive oil
- 5 slices thinly sliced bacon
- 1 teaspoon Pete's Western Rub (page 169) or salt and pepper

Instructions:

- Snap off the woody ends of asparagus and trim so they are all about the same length.
- Divide the asparagus into bundles of 3 spears and spritz with olive oil. Wrap each bundle with 1 piece of bacon and then dust with the seasoning or salt and pepper to taste.
- Configure your wood pellet smoker-grill for indirect cooking, placing Teflon coated fiberglass mats on top of the grates (to prevent the asparagus from sticking to the grill grates). Preheat to 400°F using any type of pellets. The grill can be preheated while prepping the asparagus.
- Grill the bacon-wrapped asparagus for 25 to 30 minutes, until the asparagus is tender and the bacon is cooked and crispy.

2.4 Brisket Baked Beans
Ingredients:

- 2 tablespoons extra-virgin olive oil 1 large yellow onion, diced
- 1 medium green bell pepper, diced
- 1 medium red bell pepper, diced
- 2 to 6 jalapeño peppers, diced
- 3 cups chopped Texas-Style Brisket Flat (page 91) 1 (28-ounce) can baked beans, like Bush's Country
- Style Baked Beans 1 (28-ounce) can pork and beans
- 1 (14-ounce) can red kidney beans, rinsed and drained 1 cup barbecue sauce, like Sweet Baby Ray's
- Barbecue Sauce ½ cup packed brown sugar
- 3 garlic cloves, chopped
- 2 teaspoons ground mustard
- ½ teaspoon kosher salt
- ½ teaspoon black pepper

Instructions:

- In a skillet over medium heat, warm the olive oil and then add the diced onion, peppers, and jalapeños. Cook until the onions are translucent, about 8 to 10 minutes, stirring occasionally.
- In a 4-quart casserole dish, mix the chopped brisket, baked beans, pork and beans, kidney beans, cooked onion and peppers, barbecue sauce, brown sugar, garlic, ground mustard, salt, and black pepper.
- Configure your wood pellet smoker-grill for indirect cooking and preheat to 325°F using your pellets of choice. Cook the brisket baked beans uncovered for 1½ to 2 hours, until the beans are thick and bubbly. Allow to rest for 15 minutes before serving.

2.5 Garlic Parmesan Wedges
Ingredients:

- 3 large russet potatoes
- ¼ cup extra-virgin olive oil
- 1½ teaspoons salt
- ¾ teaspoon black pepper
- 2 teaspoons garlic powder
- ¾ cup grated Parmesan cheese
- 3 tablespoons chopped fresh cilantro or flat-leaf parsley (optional)
- ½ cup blue cheese or ranch dressing per serving, for dipping (optional)

Instructions:

- Gently scrub the potatoes with cold water using a vegetable brush and allow the potatoes to dry.
- Cut the potatoes lengthwise in half, then cut those halves into thirds.
- Use a paper towel to wipe away all the moisture that is released when you cut the potatoes. Moisture prevents the wedges from getting crispy.
- Place the potato wedges, olive oil, salt, pepper, and garlic powder in a large bowl, and toss lightly with your hands, making sure the oil and spices are distributed evenly.
- Arrange the wedges in a single layer on a nonstick grilling tray/pan/basket (about 15 × 12 inches).
- Configure your wood pellet smoker-grill for indirect cooking and preheat to 425°F using any type of wood pellets.
- Place the grilling tray in your preheated smoker-grill and roast the potato wedges for 15 minutes before turning. Roast the potato wedges for an additional 15 to 20 minutes until potatoes are fork tender on the inside and crispy golden brown on the outside.
- Sprinkle the potato wedges with Parmesan cheese and garnish with cilantro or parsley, if desired. Serve with blue cheese or ranch dressing for dipping, if desired.

2.6 Roasted Vegetables
Ingredients:

- 1 cup cauliflower florets
- 1 cup small mushrooms, halved
- 1 medium zucchini, sliced and halved
- 1 medium yellow squash, sliced and halved
- 1 medium red bell pepper, chopped into 1½ to 2-inch pieces 1 small red onion, chopped into 1½ to 2- inch pieces
- 6 ounces small baby carrots
- 6 medium stemmed asparagus spears, cut into 1-inch pieces
- 1 cup cherry or grape tomatoes
- ¼ cup roasted garlic–flavored extra-virgin olive oil
- 2 tablespoons balsamic vinegar
- 3 garlic cloves, minced
- 1 teaspoon dried thyme
- 1 teaspoon dried oregano
- 1 teaspoon garlic salt
- ½ teaspoon black pepper

Instructions:

- Place the cauliflower florets, mushrooms, zucchini, yellow squash, red bell pepper, red onion, carrots, asparagus, and tomatoes into a large bowl.
- Add olive oil, balsamic vinegar, garlic, thyme, oregano, garlic salt, and black pepper to the vegetables.
- Gently hand toss the vegetables until they are fully coated with olive oil, herbs, and spices.
- Evenly scatter the seasoned vegetables onto a nonstick grilling tray/pan/basket (about 15 × 12 inches).
- Configure your wood pellet smoker-grill for indirect cooking and preheat to 425°F using any type of wood pellets.
- Transfer the grilling tray to the preheated smoker-grill and roast the vegetables for 20 to 40 minutes, or until the vegetables are al dente. Serve immediately.

2.7 Twice-Baked Spaghetti Squash
Ingredients:

- 1 medium spaghetti squash
- 1 tablespoon extra-virgin olive oil
- 1 teaspoon salt
- ½ teaspoon pepper
- ½ cup shredded mozzarella cheese, divided
- ½ cup grated Parmesan cheese, divided

Instructions:

- Carefully cut the squash in half lengthwise using a large, sharp knife. Remove the seeds and pulp of each half using a spoon.
- Rub olive oil over the insides of the squash halves and sprinkle with salt and pepper.
- Configure your wood pellet smoker-grill for indirect cooking and preheat to 375°F using any type of wood pellets.
- Place the squash halves face-up directly on the hot grill grates.
- Bake the squash for approximately 45 minutes, until the internal temperature reaches 170°F. When done, the spaghetti squash will be soft and easily pierced with a fork.
- Transfer the squash to a cutting board and allow to cool for 10 minutes.
- Increase the wood pellet smoker-grill temperature to 425°F.
- Being careful to keep the shells intact, use a fork to rake back and forth across the squash to remove the flesh in strands. Note that the stands look like spaghetti.
- Transfer the strands to a large bowl. Add half the mozzarella and Parmesan cheeses, and stir to combine.
- Stuff the mixture back in the squash shell halves, and sprinkle the tops with the remaining mozzarella and Parmesan cheeses.
- Bake the stuffed spaghetti squash halves for another 15 minutes at 425°F, or until the cheese starts to brown.

2.8 Applewood-Smoked Cheese
Ingredients:

- 1 to 2½-pound block of the following suggested cheeses: Gouda
- sharp cheddar
- extra-sharp 3-year cheddar
- Monterey Jack
- pepper Jack
- Swiss

Instructions:

- Depending on the shape of the cheese blocks, cut the cheese blocks into manageable sizes (about 4 × 4-inch blocks) to enhance smoke penetration.
- Allow the cheese to rest uncovered on the counter for 1 hour to allow a very thin skin or crust to form that acts as a barrier to heat but allows the smoke to penetrate.
- Configure your wood pellet smoker-grill for indirect heat and prepare for cold-smoking by installing a cold-smoke box. Ensure smoker box louver vents are fully open to allow moisture to escape from the box.
- Preheat your wood pellet smoker-grill to 180°F, or use the smoke setting if you have one, using apple pellets for a milder smoke flavor.
- Place the cheese on Teflon-coated fiberglass nonstick grill mats, and cold smoke for 2 hours.
- Remove the smoked cheese and allow to cool for an hour on the counter using a cooling rack.
- Vacuum-seal and label your smoked cheeses before refrigerating for a minimum of 2 weeks to allow the smoke to penetrate and for the flavor of the cheese to mellow.

2.9 Hickory-Smoked Moink Ball Skewers
Ingredients:

- ½ pound ground beef (80% lean)
- ½ pound ground pork sausage
- 1 large egg
- ½ cup Italian bread crumbs
- ½ cup minced red onions
- ½ cup grated Parmesan cheese

- ¼ cup finely chopped parsley
- ¼ cup whole milk
- 2 garlic cloves, minced, or 1 teaspoon crushed garlic 1 teaspoon oregano
- ½ teaspoon kosher salt
- ½ teaspoon black pepper
- ¼ cup barbecue sauce, like Sweet Baby Ray's ½ pound thinly sliced bacon, cut in half PREPPING

Instructions:

- In a large bowl, combine the ground beef, ground pork sausage, egg, bread crumbs, onion, Parmesan cheese, parsley, milk, garlic, salt, oregano, and pepper. Do not overwork the meat.
- Form 1½-ounce meatballs, approximately 1½ inches in diameter, and place on a Teflon-coated fiberglass mat.
- Wrap each meatball with half a slice of thin bacon. Spear the Moink balls onto 6 skewers (3 balls per skewer).
- Configure your wood pellet smoker-grill for indirect cooking.
- Preheat your wood pellet smoker-grill to 225°F using hickory pellets.
- Smoke the Moink ball skewers for 30 minutes.
- Increase your pit temperature to 350°F until the meatballs' internal temperature reaches 175°F and the bacon is crispy (approximately 40 to 45 minutes).
- Brush the Moink balls with your favorite barbecue sauce during the last 5 minutes.
- Serve the Moink ball skewers while they're still hot.

2.10 Traeger Smoked Jalapeno Poppers
Ingredients:

- 12 jalapeño peppers
- 8-ounces cream cheese, room temperature
- 10 pieces of bacon

Instructions:

- Preheat your Traeger or another wood-pellet grill to 350°.
- Wash and cut the tops off of the peppers, and then slice them in half the long way. Scrape the seeds and the membranes out, and set aside.
- Spoon softened cream cheese into the popper, and wrap with bacon and secure with a toothpick.
- Place on wire racks that are non-stick or have been sprayed with non-stick spray, and grill for 20-25 minutes, or until the bacon is cooked.

2.11 Smokey Meatball Appetizer
Ingredients:

- 1 lb. lean ground hamburger
- 1/3 C panko bread crumbs
- ½ C finely grated parmesan
- ½ C shredded old cheddar or asiago cheese
- 1 Tbsp garlic powder
- 1 Tbsp onion powder
- 1 Tbsp brown sugar
- 1 tsp kosher salt
- ½ tsp smoked paprika
- ¼ tsp chili powder
- ¼ tsp chipotle powder
- 1/8 tsp cumin
- ½ C onion, finely diced
- 1 jalapeño, finely diced
- 1 large egg, lightly beaten
- 1/8 C Worcestershire
- ½ C BBQ sauce
- 1/3" cubes of aged cheddar or asiago cheese

Instructions:

- Pre-heat the Memphis Pellet Grill to 225 F.
- Mix all of the **Ingredients:** together, except for the cheese cubes and BBQ sauce, in the order given, until everything is evenly incorporated.
- Make 1 ½" meatballs by rolling a small portion of the mixture between the palms of your hands. You will have approximately 30 meatballs when done.
- Press one cheese cube down into the center of each meatball. Once again roll each of the meatballs around, between the palms of your hands, to seal the cube of cheese inside.
- Put the cheese filled meatballs on a flat pan lined with parchment paper. Place the pan on the bottom grate of the pre-heated Memphis Grill. Close the lid and smoke for a half-hour.
- Baste the meatballs with your favorite BBQ Sauce. Close the lid and continue smoking for another half-hour. Baste again then turn the Memphis up to 350 F and close the lid. Bake for another 20 – 25 minutes. The meatballs are done when the internal temperature reaches 160 F.

2.12 Cold Smoked Cheese Easy Brie Appetizer
Ingredients:

- 21 ounces Brie cheese wheel (brought to room temperature)

Instructions:

To Smoke:

- Fill your smoker container with your choice of pellets.
- Place inside your grill, and ignite. Close the lid for a few minutes to create some smoke.
- Place the room temperature cheese on the grill (not near the smoker container).
- Close the lid, and smoke until your desired level of flavor. We smoked ours for about 80 minutes. **NOTE** Be sure the internal temperature of your grill stays under 90°F...YOU DON'T WANT TO COOK/MELT THE CHEESE.
- When done, remove from grill.
- Place on a board, along with a cheese knife, crackers, meats, and toppings.

2.13 Smoked Tomatoes on The Traeger Grill
Ingredients:

- Tomatoes, cut in half
- Dried lovage (optional)
- Sea salt
- Black pepper

- Olive oil (enough to coat the tomatoes)

Instructions:

- Set your Traeger Grill to the Smoke setting.
- Slice tomatoes in half and coat with olive oil in a bowl large enough to hold them. Add a liberal pinch of sea salt, freshly cracked black pepper, and dried lovage to taste (if using). Use your hands and mix the tomatoes until evenly coated in the mixture.
- Place tomatoes on a baking sheet and then on the Traeger Grill.
- Increase temperature to about 180-200.
- Tomatoes will be done in approximately 45 minutes. The edges will begin to curl and insides to bubble.

2.14 Smoked Olives
Ingredients:

- 1 cup black olives such as Greek Kalamata or Atalante, drained lightly
- 1 cup green olives, drained lightly
- 2 tbs extra-virgin olive oil
- 2 tbs white wine - vermouth works great
- 2 garlic cloves minced
- 3/4 tsp dried rosemary We have also used oregano with some great success but the rosemary has a better all-around taste.
- fresh ground black pepper to taste
- Perfect Mix Pellets

Instructions:

- Set pellet grill at 220 with perfect mix pellets.
- Arrange the olives in a shallow piece of heavy-duty foil molded into a small tray.
- Add the remaining **Ingredients:**
- Place the olives in the smoker and cook until the olives absorb half of the liquid and take on a light but identifiable smoke flavor, 30-50 minutes. Time depends on your grill!! Taste test after about 15-20 minutes.
- The olives can be served immediately with some asiago grated cheese over them or can sit for several hours to develop the flavor further.
- Refrigerate any leftovers. Be sure to save the leftover olive oil for bread dipping.

2.15 Classic Banana Bread
Ingredients:

- 2 cups all-purpose flour
- 3/4 teaspoon baking soda
- 1/2 teaspoon salt
- 1 cup sugar
- 1/4 cup butter, softened
- 2 large eggs
- 1 1/2 cups mashed ripe banana (about 3 bananas)
- 1/3 cup plain low-fat yogurt
- 1 teaspoon vanilla extract Cooking spray

Instructions:

- Preheat oven to 350°.
- Lightly spoon flour into dry measuring cups; level with a knife. Combine the flour, baking soda, and salt, stirring with a whisk.
- Place sugar and butter in a large bowl, and beat with a mixer at medium speed until well blended (about 1 minute). Add the eggs, 1 at a time, beating well after each addition. Add banana, yogurt, and vanilla; beat until blended. Add flour mixture; beat at low speed just until moist. Spoon batter into an 8 1/2 x 4 1/2-inch loaf pan coated with cooking spray.
- Bake at 350° for 1 hour or until a wooden pick inserted in center comes out clean. Cool 10 minutes in pan on a wire rack; remove from pan. Cool completely on wire rack.

2.16 Spaghetti Squash with Brown Butter and Parmesan
Ingredients:

- 1 spaghetti squash, 2 1/2 to 3 lb.
- 4 Tbs. (1/2 stick) unsalted butter
- Pinch of freshly grated nutmeg
- 1/3 cup grated Parmigiano-Reggiano cheese
- Salt and freshly ground pepper, to taste

Instructions:

- Place the whole squash in a large pot and add water to cover. Bring to a boil over high heat, reduce the heat to medium-low and simmer, uncovered, until the squash can be easily pierced with a knife, about 45 minutes.

- Meanwhile, in a saucepan over medium-high heat, melt the butter and cook it until it turns brown and just begins to smoke, 3 to 4 minutes. Remove immediately from the heat and stir in the nutmeg.
- When the squash is done, drain and set aside until cool enough to handle. Cut the squash in half lengthwise and, using a fork, scrape out the seeds and discard. Place the squash halves, cut sides up, on a serving platter. Using the fork, scrape the flesh free of the skin, carefully separating it into the spaghetti-like strands that it naturally forms. Leave the strands mounded in the squash halves. If the butter has cooled, place over medium heat until hot.
- To serve, drizzle the butter evenly over the squash. Sprinkle with the cheese and season with salt and pepper. Serve immediately.

2.17 Double Smoked Ham on Pellet Grill
Ingredients:

- 1 pre-cook cured smoked ham
- 2 liters of Pepsi, Coke, or Dr. Pepper

Instructions:

- Start by preheating your grill to 500 degrees.
- Place your ham long side down on the grill for 10 -20 minutes. You want to sear the ham, on all sides of the outside. So, rotate the ham around and build a nice sear all around.
- Once your ham is fully seared place in a pan and pour some pop over the ham. This is what you will use to baste throughout the cooking process.
- Drop the heat down to 225 degrees and baste your ham every 20-30 minutes for 4 hours.
- Once the 4 hours is up, pull the ham from the grill, and slice and serve.

2.18 Grilled Peach Salsa
Ingredients:

- 4 Ripe Peaches, Halved and Pitted
- 4 Heirloom Tomatoes
- 1 Bunch Cilantro
- 1 Jalapeno, Minced
- 2 Limes, Juiced
- 2 Cloves Garlic Minced
- 2 Tbsp Olive Oil
- Salt and Pepper to Taste

Instructions:

- When ready to cook, set temperature to High and preheat, lid closed for 15 minutes.
- Brush the cut side of the peaches with olive oil and season with salt. Place the peaches, cut side down, along the perimeter of the grill. Cook for 20 minutes or so until grill marks develop. Its best to pick peaches that are not too ripe and more on the firm side.
- Remove the peaches from the grill and dice when cool enough to handle. Place in a large bowl with diced tomatoes, minced cilantro, jalapeno, lime juice, garlic and olive oil and mix well. Taste and season with salt. Adjust with more lime juice if needed. Enjoy with your favorite chips!
- Serve with chips or on your favorite dishes. Enjoy!

2.19 Pizza Bites
Ingredients:

- 4 1/2 CUPS BREAD FLOUR, PLUS MORE FOR DUSTING
- 1 1/2 TBSP SUGAR
- 2 TSP INSTANT YEAST
- 3 TBSP EXTRA-VIRGIN OLIVE OIL
- 15 OZ LUKEWARM WATER
- PIZZA FILLING
- 1 CUP MOZARELLA CHEESE
- 8 OZ PEPPERONI, CUT INTO THIN STRIPS
- 1 CUP PIZZA SAUCE
- 1 EGG FOR EGG WASH

Instructions:

- For the Pizza Dough: Combine flour, sugar, salt, and yeast in food processor. Pulse 3 to 4 times until incorporated evenly. Add olive oil and water. Run food processor until mixture forms ball that rides around the bowl above the blade, about 15 seconds. Continue processing 15 seconds longer.
- Transfer dough ball to lightly floured surface and knead once or twice by hand until smooth ball is formed. Divide dough into three even parts and place each into a 1-gallon zip top bag. Place in refrigerator and allow to rise at least one day.
- At least two hours before baking, remove dough from refrigerator and shape into balls by gathering dough towards bottom and pinching shut. Flour well and place each one in a separate medium mixing bowl. Cover tightly with plastic wrap and allow to rise at warm room temperature until roughly doubled in volume.
- When ready to cook, set the temperature to 350°F and preheat, lid closed for 15 minutes.
- After the first rise remove the dough from the fridge and let come to room temperature. Roll dough on a flat surface. Cut dough into long strips 3" wide by 18" long.
- Slice pepperoni into strips.
- In a medium bowl combine the pizza sauce, mozzarella and pepperoni.
- Spoon 1 TBSP of the pizza filling onto the pizza dough every two inches, about halfway down the length of the dough. Dip a pastry brush into the egg wash and brush around pizza filling. Fold the half side of the dough (without the pizza filling) over the other the half that contains the pizza filling.
- Press down between each pizza bite slightly with your fingers. With a ravioli or pizza cutter, cut around each filling- creating a rectangle shape and sealing the crust in.
- Transfer each pizza bite onto a parchment lined cookie sheet. Cover with a kitchen towel and let them rise for 30 minutes.
- When ready to cook, preheat the grill to 350 F with the lid closed for 10-15 minutes.

- Brush the bites with remaining egg wash, sprinkle with salt and place directly on the sheet tray. Bake 10-15 minutes until the exterior is golden brown.
- Remove from grill and transfer to a serving dish. Serve with extra pizza sauce for dipping and enjoy!

2.20 Spicy Shrimp Skewers
Ingredients:

- 2 Lbs. Shrimp, Peeled, And Deveined
- 6 Oz Thai Chilies
- 6 Cloves Garlic
- 2 Tbsp Winemakers Blend Napa Valley Rub
- 1-1/2 Tsp Sugar
- 1-1/2 Tbsp White Vinegar
- 3 Tbsp Olive Oil
- Bamboo or Metal Skewers

Instructions:

- Place all **Ingredients:** besides shrimp in a blender and blend until a course textured paste is reached.
- Place shrimp in a bowl, add chili garlic mixture and place in fridge to marinate for at least 30 minutes.
- Remove from fridge and thread shrimp onto bamboo or metal skewers.
- When ready to cook, start the Traeger according to grill instructions. Set the temperature to 450 degrees F (set to 500 degrees F if using a WiFIRE enables grill) and preheat, lid closed, for 10 to 15 minutes.
- Place shrimp on grill and cook for 2 to 3 minutes per side or until shrimp are pink and firm to touch. Enjoy!

2.21 Traeger Jerk Shrimp
Ingredients:

- 1 Tbsp Brown Sugar
- 1 Tbsp Smoked Paprika
- 1 Tsp Garlic Powder
- 1/4 Tsp Ground Thyme
- 1/4 Tsp Ground Cayenne
- 1/8 Tsp Smoked Paprika
- 1 Tsp Sea Salt
- Zest Of 1 Lime
- 3 Tbsp Olive Oil
- 2 Lbs. Shrimp, Peel On

Instructions:

- Combine spices, salt, and lime zest in a small bowl and mix. Place shrimp into a large bowl, then drizzle in the olive oil, Add the spice mixture and toss to combine, making sure every shrimp is kissed with deliciousness.
- When ready to cook, set the temperature to 450°F and preheat, lid closed for 15 minutes
- Arrange the shrimp on the grill and cook for 2 – 3 minutes per side, until firm, opaque, and cooked through.
- Serve with lime wedges, fresh cilantro, mint, and Caribbean Hot Pepper Sauce. Enjoy!

2.22 Hellfire Chicken Wings
Ingredients:

- Hellfire Chicken Wings
- 3 Lbs. Chicken Wings
- 2 Tbsp. Vegetable Oil
- Rub
- 1 Tbsp. Paprika
- 2 Tsp. Brown Sugar
- 1 Tsp. Salt
- 1 Tsp. Black Pepper, Freshly Ground
- 1 Tsp. Cayenne Pepper
- 1 Tsp. Onion Powder
- 1 Tsp. Granulated Garlic
- 1 Tsp. Celery Seed
- Sauce
- 8 Tbsp. Butter, Unsalted
- 2 - 4 Jalapeno Peppers, Thinly Sliced Crosswise
- 1/2 Cup Cilantro Leaves
- 1/2 Cup Hot Sauce

Instructions:

- Cut the tips off wings and discard. Cut each wing into two pieces through the joint, giving you a meaty "drumette" and a "flat". Transfer to a large mixing bowl and pour the oil over the chicken
- Make the rub: In a small mixing bowl, combine the paprika, sugar, salt, black pepper, cayenne, onion powder, granulated garlic, and celery seed.
- Sprinkle over the chicken and toss gently with your hands to coat the wings.
- When ready to cook, set the temperature to 350°F and preheat, lid closed for 15 minutes
- Grill the wings for 35 to 40 minutes, or until the skin is crisp and golden brown and the chicken is cooked through, turning once halfway through the cooking time.
- Make the sauce: Melt the butter over medium-low heat in a small saucepan. Add the jalapeños and cook for 3-4 minutes. Stir in the cilantro & hot sauce.
- Pour the sauce over the wings and toss to coat. Enjoy!

2.23 Grilled Bison Sliders
Ingredients:

- 1 Lb. Ground Buffalo Meat
- 3 Cloves Garlic, Minced
- 2 Tbsp Worcestershire Sauce
- 1 Tsp Salt
- 1 Tsp Black Pepper

Instructions:

- Combine the buffalo meat, garlic, Worcestershire sauce, salt and pepper in a mixing bowl. Blend together with hands.
- Form meat into 8 small patties. Place on a plate and put in fridge.
- When ready to cook, set temperature to High and preheat, lid closed for 15 minutes.
- Remove patties from fridge and place on grill. Grill patties for 4 minutes on each side and remove from grill.
- If you want to add cheese, place sliced cheese on patties the last 2 minutes of cooking to melt.
- To toast buns, place buns on grill grate the last minute of cooking.
- Serve with sliced onions, pickles, tomatoes, lettuce and condiments of your choice. Enjoy!

2.24 Smoked Jalapeño Poppers
Ingredients:

12 Medium Jalapeños

6 Slices Bacon, Cut in Half

8 Oz Cream Cheese, Softened

1 Cup Cheese, Grated

2 Tbsp Traeger Pork & Poultry Rub

Instructions:

- When ready to cook, set temperature to 180°F and preheat, lid closed for 15 minutes.
- Slice the jalapeños in half lengthwise. Scrape out any seeds and ribs with a small spoon or paring knife.
- Mix softened cream cheese with Traeger Pork & Poultry rub and grated cheese.
- Spoon mixture onto each jalapeño half. Wrap with bacon and secure with a toothpick.
- Place the jalapeños on a rimmed baking sheet. Place on grill and smoke for 30 minutes.
- Increase the grill temperature to 375°F and cook an additional 30 minutes or until bacon is cooked to desired doneness. Serve warm, enjoy!

2.25 Easy Garlic Cheese Bombs
Ingredients:

- 4 1/2 Cups Bread Flour, Plus More for Dusting
- 1 1/2 Tbsp Sugar
- 2 Tsp Instant Yeast
- 3 Tbsp Extra-Virgin Olive Oil
- 15 Oz Lukewarm Water
- Cheese Filling
- 1 Lb. Block Mozzarella Cheese
- 4 Tbsp Butter
- 1 Tsp Garlic Salt
- 1 Tbsp Shredded Parmesan Cheese

Instructions:

- For the Pizza Dough: Combine flour, sugar, salt, and yeast in food processor. Pulse 3 to 4 times until incorporated evenly. Add olive oil and water. Run food processor until mixture forms ball that rides around the bowl above the blade, about 15 seconds. Continue processing 15 seconds longer.
- Transfer dough ball to lightly floured surface and knead once or twice by hand until smooth ball is formed. Divide dough into three even parts and place each into a 1-gallon zip top bag. Place in refrigerator and allow to rise at least for 24 hours.
- At least two hours before baking, remove dough from refrigerator and shape into balls by gathering dough towards bottom and pinching shut. Flour well and place each one in a separate medium mixing bowl. Cover tightly with plastic wrap and allow to rise at warm room temperature until roughly doubled in volume.
- Roll the pizza dough out into a rectangle ¼" thick. Cut into strips 2" thick. Then again to create 2x2 squares.
- Place one piece of cheese in the center of each dough square. Brush the edges with a little bit of water and fold the edges up securing tightly.
- Place the cheese balls seam side down on a parchment lined baking sheet.
- In a small bowl combine the melted butter, garlic salt and cheese.
- Brush each cheese ball with the butter mixture.
- When ready to cook, set the temperature to 350 °F and preheat, lid closed for 10-15 minutes.
- Place the sheet tray directly on the grill grate and bake for 20-30 minutes until light brown in color. Enjoy with marinara or your favorite dipping sauce.

2.26 Traeger Baked Corn Dog Bites
Ingredients:

- 1 Cup Milk at Room Temp
- 4 Tsp Active Dry Yeast
- 1/4 Cup Granulated Sugar
- 2 Cups All-Purpose Flour
- 1/2 Cup Yellow Corn Meal
- 1 Tsp Baking Soda
- 1/2 Tsp Mustard Powder
- 1/4 Cup Vegetable Oil
- 1/2 Tsp Cayenne Pepper
- 1 Egg, Lightly Beaten
- 15 Mini Hot Dogs
- 1 Tbsp Dried Mince Garlic
- 1 Tbsp Coarse Salt
- Ketchup & Mustard for Serving

Instructions:

- When ready to cook, set the temperature to 375°F and preheat, lid closed for 15 minutes.
- Combine milk, yeast and sugar in a bowl. Set aside for 5 minutes or until it starts to foam.
- Then add oil, salt, cayenne pepper, mustard powder, baking soda, corn meal, all- purpose flour. Mix with a spoon until combined then use your hands to knead into a dough.
- Transfer dough to a bowl and cover with plastic wrap and set aside for about 45 minutes- until dough rises and doubles in size.
- Remove dough from bowl and divide into 15 pieces. On a working surface dusted with flour, use a rolling pin to roll out each piece of dough into 3" x 3" pieces. Place each hot dog in the middle of the sheet of dough. Roll it in the dough and press edges to seal to make 15 mini corn dog bites.
- Transfer corn dog bites into a baking pan lined with parchment paper and brush each bite lightly with beaten egg. Sprinkle each bite with dried minced garlic and salt.
- Bake in Traeger until golden brown- about 30 min.
- Serve with ketchup and mustard or dipping sauce of your choice. Enjoy!

2.27 Baked Heirloom Tomato Tart
Ingredients:

- 1 Sheet Puff Pastry
- 2 Lbs. Heirloom Tomatoes, Various Shapes and Sizes
- 1/2 Cup Ricotta
- 5 Eggs
- 1/2 Tbsp Kosher Salt
- 1/2 Tsp Thyme Leaves
- 1/2 Tsp Red Pepper Flakes
- Pinch of Black Pepper
- 4 Sprigs Thyme
- Salt and Pepper, To Taste

Instructions:

- When ready to cook, set temperature to 350°F and preheat, lid closed for 15 minutes.
- Place the puff pastry on a parchment lined sheet tray, and make a cut ¾ of the way through the pastry, ½" from the edge.
- Slice the tomatoes and season with salt. Place on a sheet tray lined with paper towels.
- In a small bowl combine the ricotta, 4 of the eggs, salt, thyme leaves, red pepper flakes and black pepper. Whisk together until combined. Spread the ricotta mixture over the puff pastry, staying within ½" from the edge.
- Lay the tomatoes out on top of the ricotta, and sprinkle with salt, pepper and thyme sprigs.
- In a small bowl whisk the last egg. Brush the egg wash onto the exposed edges of the pastry.
- Place the sheet tray directly on the grill grate and bake for 45 minutes, rotating half-way through.
- When the edges are browned and the moisture from the tomatoes has evaporated, remove from the grill and let cool 5-7 minutes before serving. Enjoy!

2.28 Grilled Piña Colada
Ingredients:

- 7.5 Oz Light Rum
- 2 Oz Dark Rum
- 15 Oz Coconut Milk
- 1 Pineapple, Trimmed, Cored and Cut into Spears
- 5 Cups Ice

Instructions:

- When ready to cook, set temperature to High and preheat, lid closed for 15 minutes.
- Grill pineapple spears 10 minutes until lightly browned.
- Combine 3/4 of the grilled pineapple, coconut milk and both rums in the pitcher of a blender. Add ice and blend until smooth.
- Divide blender contents into four glasses and garnish with remaining grilled pineapple. Enjoy!

2.29 BBQ Chicken Nachos
Ingredients:

- 1-1/4 Lbs. Chicken Breasts, Boneless, Skinless
- Traeger Pork & Poultry Rub, As Needed
- 1/2 To 3/4 Cup Traeger Qu BBQ Sauce
- 24 Large Tortilla Chips
- 3 Cups Mexican Blend Shredded Cheese
- 1/2 Cup Black Olives, Sliced and Drained
- Pickled Jalapenos, Sliced
- 3 Scallions, Thinly Sliced
- 1 Cup Sour Cream

Instructions:

- Season the chicken breasts with the Traeger Pork and Poultry Rub.
- When ready to cook, set temperature to 350°F and preheat, lid closed for 15 minutes.
- Arrange the chicken breasts on the grill grate and cook, turning once halfway through the cooking time, for 25 to 30 minutes, or until the internal temperature when read on an instant-read meat thermometer is 170°F. Transfer to a cutting board and let rest for 3 minutes. Leave the grill on if you are making the nachos immediately.
- Dice the chicken into small cubes, 1/2-inch or less. Transfer to a mixing bowl and pour 1/2 cup of Traeger Regular Barbecue Sauce over the diced chicken. Stir gently to coat each piece.
- Set aside, or cover and refrigerate if not making the nachos immediately. Lay the tortilla chips in a single layer on a rimmed baking sheet or pizza pan. Sprinkle evenly with half the cheese and a few of the jalapenos (if using).
- Spoon barbecued chicken mixture on each chip. Top with black olives and more pickled jalapeno, if desired. Sprinkle the remaining half of the cheese evenly over the chips. Scatter the sliced onions over the chips.
- Put the baking sheet on the grill grate. Bake until the chips are crisp and the cheese is melted, 12 to 15 minutes. With a spatula, transfer the nachos to a plate or platter. Serve immediately with sour cream and pickled jalapenos. Enjoy!

2.30 Chinese BBQ Pork
Ingredients:

- Pork & Marinade
- 2 Pork Tenderloins, Silver Skin Removed
- 1/4 Cup Hoisin Sauce
- 1/4 Cup Honey
- 1 1/2 Tbsp Brown Sugar
- 3 Tbsp Soy Sauce
- 1 Tbsp Asian Sesame Oil
- 1 Tbsp Oyster Sauce, Optional
- 1 Tsp Chinese Five Spice
- 1 Garlic Clove, Minced
- 2 Tsp Red Food Coloring, Optional
- Five Spice Dipping Sauce
- 1/4 Cup Ketchup
- 3 Tbsp Brown Sugar
- 1 Tsp Yellow Mustard
- 1/4 Tsp Chinese Five Spice

Instructions:

- In medium bowl, whisk together marinade **Ingredients:** thoroughly, making sure brown sugar is dissolved. Add pork and marinade to glass pan or resealable plastic bag and marinate for at least 8 hours or overnight, turning occasionally to ensure all sides of pork are well coated.
- When ready to cook, set the temperature to 225°F and preheat, lid closed for 15 minutes.
- Remove pork from marinade and boil marinade in a saucepan over medium high heat on stove top for 3 minutes to use for basting pork. Cool slightly, then whisk in 2 additional Tablespoons of honey.
- Arrange the tenderloins on the grill grate and smoke pork until internal temperature reaches 145°F.
- Baste pork with reserved marinade half way through cooking. Remove pork from grill and, if desired, increase temperature to High and return pork to grill for a few minutes per side to slightly char and set the sauce. Alternatively, you can broil in the oven, just a couple minutes per side.
- For the 5 Spice Sauce: In a small saucepan over low heat, mix ketchup, brown sugar, mustard and five spice until sugar is dissolved and sauce is smooth. Let cool, and serve chilled or at room temperature.
- Serve pork immediately with Jasmine rice, or cool and refrigerate for later use as an appetizer, served with Five Spice dipping sauce and toasted sesame seeds. Enjoy!

2.31 Smoked Pickled Green Beans
Ingredients:

- 1 Lb. Green Beans, Blanched
- 1/2 Cup Salt
- 1/2 Cup Sugar
- 1 Tbsp Red Pepper Flake
- 2 Cups White Wine Vinegar
- 2 Cups Ice Water

Instructions:

- When ready to cook, set temperature to 180°F and preheat, lid closed for 15 minutes.
- Place the blanched green beans on a mesh grill mat and place mat directly on the grill grate. Smoke the green beans for 30-45 minutes until they've picked up the desired amount of smoke. Remove from grill and set aside until the brine is ready.
- In a medium sized saucepan, bring all remaining **Ingredients:** except ice water, to a boil over medium high heat on the stove. Simmer for 5-10 minutes then remove from heat and steep 20 minutes more. Pour brine over ice water to cool.
- Once brine has cooled, pour over the green beans and weigh them down with a few plates to ensure they are completely submerged. Let sit 24 hours before use.

2.32 Seared Lemon Garlic Scallops
- **Ingredients:**
- Scallops
- 1 Dozen U-20 Scallops
- Kosher Salt
- 1 Tbsp Butter
- 1 Tbsp Olive Oil
- Chopped Parsley, To Garnish
- Lemon Zest, To Garnish
- Garlic Butter
- 4 Tbsp Butter, Melted
- Juice Of 1 Lemon
- 1 Clove Garlic, Minced

Instructions:

- When ready to cook, set the temperature to 400°F and preheat, lid closed for 15 minutes.
- Remove the frill if it is still intact. Pat the scallops dry with a paper towel. Season liberally with salt and a bit of black pepper.
- When the grill is hot, place the butter and olive oil on the skillet. When the butter has melted, place the scallops on the skillet. Close the lid and cook for about 2 minutes until seared and browned on one side.
- While the scallops cook, combine the melted butter and garlic in a small bowl.
- Flip the scallops, spoon a couple tablespoons of garlic butter over the top and cook for 1 minute longer.
- Remove from the grill, add a little more garlic butter if desired and finish with parsley and lemon zest.

2.33 Baked Asparagus Pancetta Cheese Tart
Ingredients:

- 1 Sheet Puff Pastry
- 8 Oz Asparagus, Pencil Spears
- 8 Oz Pancetta, Cooked and Drained
- 1 Cup Cream
- 4 Eggs
- 1/4 Cup Goat Cheese
- 4 Tbsp Grated Parmesan
- 1 Tbsp Chopped Chives
- Black Pepper

Instructions:

- When ready to cook, set the temperature to 375°F and preheat, lid closed for 15 minutes.
- Place the puff pastry on a half sheet tray and score around the perimeter 1-inch in from the edges making sure not to cut all the way through. Prick the center of the puff pastry with a fork.
- Place the sheet tray directly on the grill grate and bake for 15-20 minutes until the pastry has puffed and browned a little bit.
- While the pastry bakes combine the cream, 3 eggs, both cheeses and chives in a small bowl. Whisk to mix well.
- Remove the sheet tray from the grill and pour the egg mixture into the puff pastry. Lay the asparagus spears on top of the egg mixture and sprinkle with cooked pancetta.
- Whisk remaining egg in a small bowl and brush the top of the pastry with the egg wash.
- Place back on the grill grate and cook for another 15-20 minutes until the egg mixture is just set.
- Finish tart with lemon zest, more chopped chives and shaved parmesan.

2.34 Smoked Deviled Eggs
Ingredients:

- 7 Hard Boiled Eggs, Cooked and Peeled
- 3 Tbsp Mayonnaise
- 3 Tsp Chives, Diced
- 1 Tsp Brown Mustard
- 1 Tsp Apple Cider Vinegar
- Dash of Hot Sauce
- Salt and Pepper, To Taste
- 2 Tbsp Bacon, Crumbled
- Paprika, For Dusting

Instructions:

- When ready to cook, set temperature to 180°F and preheat, lid closed for 15 minutes. For optimal flavor, use Super Smoke if available.
- Place cooked and peeled eggs directly on the grill grate and smoke eggs for 30 minutes. Remove from grill and allow eggs to cool.
- Slice the eggs lengthwise and scoop the egg yolks into a gallon zip top bag. Add mayonnaise, chives, mustard, vinegar, hot sauce, salt, and pepper to the bag.
- Zip the bag closed and, using your hands, knead all of the **Ingredients:** together until completely smooth.
- Squeeze the yolk mixture into one corner of the bag and cut a small part of the corner off. Pipe the yolk mixture into the hardboiled egg whites.
- Top the deviled eggs with crumbled bacon and paprika. Chill until ready to serve. Enjoy!

2.35 Baked Soft Pretzel with Beer Cheese Sauce
Ingredients:

- Soft Pretzel
- 1 1/2 Cups Warm Water (110-115°F)
- 1 Tbsp Sugar
- 1 Package Active Dry Yeast

- 4 1/2 Cups All Purpose Flour
- 2 Tbsp Kosher Salt
- 2 Oz Melted Unsalted Butter
- Cooking Oil Spray
- 10 Cups Water
- 2/3 Cup Baking Soda
- 1 Large Egg Yolk Beaten With 1 Tbsp Water
- Jacobsen Smoked Sea Salt, As Needed
- Beer Cheese Sauce
- 2 Cups Sharp Cheddar Cheese
- 1/2 Cup Cream Cheese, Room Temperature
- 1/2 Tbsp Worcestershire Sauce
- 2 Tsp Dijon Mustard
- 2 Cloves Garlic, Minced
- 1 Tsp Paprika
- 1/2 Cup Beer

Instructions:

- In the bowl of a stand mixer, combine the water and sugar and sprinkle the dry yeast on top. Let it sit for 5-6 minutes until it starts to foam on top.
- Add flour, salt, and butter to the bowl, and with the hook attachment mix on low until well combined. Then mix on medium for about 5 minutes until dough is smooth and pulls away from the sides.
- Remove dough from bowl and spray bowl well with cooking oil spray. Return dough to the bowl, cover with a cloth or plastic wrap and allow the dough to double in size.
- When ready to cook, set the Traeger to 350°F and preheat, lid closed for 15 minutes.
- While dough rises, bring to a boil 10 cups of water and the baking soda.
- When dough is ready, divide into 8 pieces. Roll each piece into a 24-inch rope.
- Form a U shape with each rope, holding each end of the rope and cross them over each other and press it down on the bottom of the U forming a pretzel.
- One by one, place each pretzel in the boiling water for 30 seconds. With a flat spatula take them out and place in a sheet pan.
- Brush pretzels with egg yolk and sprinkle with smoked sea salt. Bake in the Traeger for about 25-30 minutes.
- To make the Beer Cheese Sauce: In a food processor bowl, add cheddar cheese, cream cheese, Worcestershire sauce, Dijon mustard, garlic and paprika. Blend until finely chopped, add the beer slowly until is smooth.
- When pretzels are done serve with the beer cheese sauce. Enjoy!

2.36 Bacon Grilled Cheese Sandwich
Ingredients:

- 1 Lb. Applewood Smoked Bacon Slices, Cooked
- 8 Slices Texas Toast
- 16 Slices Cheddar Cheese
- Mayonnaise
- Butter

Instructions:

- When ready to cook, set the temperature to 350°F and preheat, lid closed for 15 minutes.
- Spread a little bit of mayonnaise on each piece of bread, place 1 piece of cheddar on a slice then top with a couple slices of bacon. Add another slice of cheese then top with the other piece of bread. Spread softened butter on the exterior of the top piece of bread.
- When the grill is hot, place the grilled cheese directly on a cleaned, oiled grill grate buttered side down. Then spread softened butter on the exterior of the top slice.
- Cook the grilled cheese on the first side 5-7 minutes until grill marks develop and the cheese has begun to melt. Flip the sandwich and repeat on the other side.
- Remove from the grill when the cheese is melted and the exterior is lightly toasted. Enjoy!

2.37 Stuffed Avocados
Ingredients:

- 4 Avocados, Halved, Pit Removed
- 8 Eggs
- 2 Cups Shredded Cheddar Cheese
- 4 Slices Bacon, Cooked and Chopped
- 1/4 Cup Cherry Tomatoes, Halved
- Green Onions, Sliced Thin
- Salt and Pepper, To Taste

Instructions:

- When ready to cook, set the temperature to High and preheat, lid closed for 15 minutes.
- After removing the pit from the avocado, scoop out a little of the flesh to make enough room to fit 1 egg per half.
- Fill the bottom of a cast iron pan with kosher salt and nestle the avocado halves into the salt, cut side up. The salt helps to keep them in place while cooking, like ice with oysters.
- Crack egg into each half, top with a hand full of shredded cheddar cheese, some cherry tomatoes and bacon. Season with salt and pepper to taste.
- Place the cast iron pan directly on the grill grate and bake the avocados for 12-15 minutes until the cheese is melted and the egg is just set.
- Remove from the grill and let rest 5-10 minutes. Enjoy!

2.38 Braised Backstrap Shredded Tacos
Ingredients:

- 4 Tbsp Grass Fed Butter
- 3 Cloves Fresh Garlic
- 4 Lbs. Large Cuts of Wild Game Neck, Shoulder or Arm Meat
- 3/4 Cup Bone Broth
- 2 Tbsp Traeger Prime Rib Rub
- 2 Tbsp Traeger Coffee Rub
- Sugar Lips Sriracha BBQ Glaze
- 4 Jalapeños
- 20 Tortillas
- 2 Bunches Cilantro, Chopped
- 3 Avocados, Sliced

Instructions:

- When ready to cook, set the temperature to 250°F and preheat, lid closed for 15 minutes
- Add the grass-fed butter and garlic to a large Dutch oven and place on the stovetop. Add the game meat to the Dutch oven and sear on all sides.
- Remove from heat and season with Traeger Prime Rib and Traeger Coffee rubs.
- Add the bone broth to the pot and cover. Wrap the seam of the lids tightly with foil.
- Place directly on the grill grate and cook for approximately 8 hours without peeking.
- Remove the lid and twist the meat with a fork. If the meat easily shreds, then drizzle Sriracha Sugar Lips on top and cover with the lid. If the meat doesn't fall apart yet, recover and continue to cook for another hour or until tender.
- Reduce grill temperature to 180°F. Place jalapeños directly on the grill grate and smoke the peppers for 20 minutes.
- With 10 minutes remaining, wrap a stack of tortillas in foil and set them in the Traeger to warm
- Remove Dutch oven from the grill and shred meat with two large forks. Mix in another drizzle of Sriracha Sugar Lips and cover pot.
- Remove tortillas and jalapeños from the grill and slice jalapeños.
- Build tacos with shredded backstrap, jalapeños and avocados. Garnish with cilantro. Enjoy!

Chapter 3: Beef Recipes

3.1 Blackened Saskatchewan Tomahawk Steak
Ingredients:

- 2 (40 Oz) Tomahawk Steaks
- 4 Tbsp Butter
- 4 Tbsp Blackened Saskatchewan Rub

Instructions:

- When ready to cook, set temperature to 225°F and preheat, lid closed for 15 minutes. For optimal flavor, use Super Smoke if available.
- Cover cold steaks in the Blackened Saskatchewan Rub. Let rest 10 minutes for the seasoning to adhere.
- Place steaks directly on grill grates and smoke for about 40 minutes, or until an internal temp reaches 119°F. Remove from grill and wrap tightly in foil to rest.
- Turn up temperature on the grill to 400°F- with a cast iron pan or griddle inside. When the pan is hot, add 2 Tbsp of butter and sear the first steak, about 2-4 minutes per side, or until the internal temperature reads 125°F - 130°F. Repeat with the other Tomahawk. Rest, slice, serve. Enjoy!

3.2 Traeger BBQ Brisket
Ingredients:

- 1 (12-14 Lb.) Whole Packer Brisket
- Traeger Beef Rub, As Needed

Instructions:

- Coat meat liberally with Traeger Beef Rub. When seasoned, wrap brisket in plastic wrap. Let the wrapped meat sit 12 to 24 hours in the refrigerator.
- When ready to cook, set the Traeger to 225°F and preheat, lid closed for 15 minutes.
- Place meat fat side down on the grill grate and cook for 6 hours or until internal temperature reaches 160°F. Remove brisket from the grill and wrap in foil.
- Place foiled brisket back on grill and cook until it reaches a finished internal temperature of 204°F this should take an additional 3-4 hours.
- Remove from grill and allow to rest in the foil for at least 30 minutes. Slice. Enjoy!

3.3 Garlic, Lemon, And Goat Cheese Mashed Potatoes
Ingredients:

- 1 Head of Garlic
- 1 Tsp Olive Oil
- 3 Lbs. Yukon Gold Potatoes, Peeled and Roughly Chopped
- 3/4 Cup Crumbled Goat Cheese
- 1/4 Cup Melted Butter, Plus More for Drizzling
- 3/4 Cup Heavy Whipping Cream
- Sea Salt & Freshly Cracked Black Pepper
- 2 Tbs Fresh Chives, Finely Diced

Instructions:

- When ready to cook, set the temperature to 350°F and preheat, lid closed, for 10 to 15 minutes.
- Using a sharp knife, slice about ⅛" off the top of the garlic head (leaving the root intact), exposing the individual garlic cloves. Drizzle the olive oil on top of the exposed garlic and season with a pinch of salt and pepper. Tightly wrap the bulb in aluminum foil and roast on the Traeger for 30 - 35 minutes, until the cloves are soft. Remove the garlic cloves and mash into a paste with a fork.
- Meanwhile, bring a large stockpot of salted water to a boil over medium high heat. Add the potatoes and cook for 15 - 20 minutes, or until softened and hashable. Drain and return to the pot, stirring until dry. Remove from the heat and stir in the cream, goat cheese, lemon zest, garlic mash, and ¼ cup of butter. Mash until smooth, and if you like it, whip that business up with a whisk. Season with salt and pepper to taste. Garnish with extra chives and a generous drizzle of melted butter. Enjoy!

3.4 Traeger Prime Rib Roast
Ingredients:

- 1 (5-7 Bones) Prime Rib Roast
- Traeger Prime Rib Rub, As Needed

Instructions:

- Coat the roast evenly with the Traeger Prime Rib Rub and wrap in plastic wrap. Let sit in the refrigerator for 24 hours.
- When ready to cook, set the temperature to High and preheat, lid closed for 15 minutes.
- Place the prime rib fat side up, directly on the grill grate and cook for 30 minutes. Starting at a higher heat will help to develop a crispy, rendered crust.
- After 30 minutes, reduce the grill temperature to 325°F.
- Close lid and roast at 325°F for 3-4 hours or until cooked to desired internal temperature, 120°F for rare, 130°F for medium rare, 140°F for medium and 150°F for well done.
- Remove from grill and let rest 15 minutes before carving. Enjoy!

3.5 Italian Beef Sandwich
Ingredients:

- 1 Qty. (4 Lb.) Lean, Boneless Beef Roast (Sirloin or Top Round)
- Salt
- Pepper
- 4 Cloves Garlic, Thinly Sliced
- Traeger Prime Rib Rub
- 6 Cups Beef Broth
- 8 Hoagie-Style Buns (For Sandwiches)
- 6 Slices Swiss Cheese
- 1 Cup Bottled Giardiniera (Italian Pickled Vegetables; Optional), Chopped

Instructions:

- When ready to cook, set the temperature to 450°F and preheat, lid closed for 15 minutes.
- Season the roast liberally with salt, pepper and Traeger prime rib rub. Using a paring knife, make 10-15 slits in the roast every 1" or so. Insert a garlic clove into each slit.
- Place the roast directly on the grill grate and cook for about 1 hour flipping halfway through until browned well.
- Remove the roast from the grill and transfer to a deep Dutch oven. Pour the beef broth over the roast. Cover tightly with foil and place back on the grill. Reduce the grill temperature to 300°F and cook the roast for 3-4 hours or until it is fork tender.
- While the roast cooks, chop the giardiniera into small pieces.
- Remove the Dutch oven from the grill and shred removing any large bits of fat or connective tissue. Transfer the meat back to the Dutch over and stir to combine with the juices.
- Increase the grill temperature to high and preheat lid closed for 10 minutes.
- Place hoagie buns cut side up on a small sheet tray. Fill with the shredded roast and top with a slice of cheese. Transfer to the grill and cook for another 5-10 minutes or until the cheese is melted.
- Remove from the grill and top with chopped pickled veggies. Serve with remaining cooking liquid for dipping if desired. Enjoy!

3.6 Thai Beef Skewers
Ingredients:

- 1/4 Cup Vegetable Oil
- 1/4 Cup Soy Sauce
- 1 Juice of Lime
- 2 Cloves Garlic, Finely Minced
- 1 Tbsp. Fresh Ginger, Peeled and Minced
- 1 Tsp. Black Pepper, Freshly Ground
- 1/2 Beef Sirloin, Trimmed and Cut Into 1-1/4 Inch Dice
- 1/2 Red Bell Pepper, Stemmed, Seeded, And Cut Into 1/4 Inch Dice
- 1/2 Cup Dry-Roasted Peanuts (Salted or Unsalted), Coarsely Chopped
- 1 Traeger Skewers Set

Instructions:

- In a small bowl, whisk together the oil, soy sauce, lime juice, garlic, ginger, sugar, and black pepper. Transfer the meat to a large bowl or resealable plastic bag and pour the marinade over the meat, turning to coat each piece thoroughly. Refrigerate for 2 to 4 hours, or longer if desired.
- Drain the marinade off the sirloin cubes (discard the marinade) and pat them dry with paper towels. Thread the meat on the skewers, keeping the pieces close together to minimize exposure of the skewer to the heat. (You can also slip a folded length of aluminum foil under the exposed ends to protect them.)
- When ready to cook, set the temperature to 425°F and preheat, lid closed for 15 minutes.
- Arrange the skewers on the grill grate and grill for 2 to 4 minutes per side, or until the desired degree of doneness is reached. To serve, sprinkle with the diced red pepper and the chopped peanuts. Enjoy!

3.7 BBQ CHILI BURGER
Ingredients:

- Beef Chili
- 2.5 Lbs. Ground Beef
- 1 Large Onion, Diced
- 1 Tsp Kosher Salt
- 1 Can Chipotles in Adobo, Minced with Sauce
- 1/4 Cup Chili Powder
- 1-1/2 Tbsp Cumin Powder
- 3 Cloves Garlic, Peeled and Minced
- 1 Jalapeño Pepper, Minced
- 1 (14 Oz) Can Diced or Crushed Tomatoes
- 2 Cups Chicken Stock
- 1/8 Cup Flour
- 1/2 Tbsp Dark Chili Powder
- 1/2 Tbsp Ground Cinnamon
- Juice Of 1 Lime
- 1 Hershey's Chocolate Bar
- Salt and Pepper, To Taste
- Chili Burgers
- 2 Lbs. Ground Beef
- Traeger Beef Rub, As Needed
- 2 Cups Beef Chili or Preferred Chili
- 5 Hamburger Buns
- 5 Slices Cheddar Cheese
- 1 Red Onion, Sliced
- 1 Bag Frito Corn Chips

Instructions:

- For the Beef Chili: Heat a large Dutch oven on the stove top over medium-high heat. Cook the ground beef until browned and cooked through.
- Add all chili **Ingredients:** minus the chocolate and limes to the Dutch oven.
- When ready to cook, start the Traeger according to grill instructions. Set the temperature to 350 degrees F and preheat, lid closed for 10 to 15 minutes.
- Put the Dutch oven into the grill for 2 hours, stirring every hour. Remove Dutch oven from grill.
- Stir the lime juice and the chocolate into the chili. Set chili aside until ready to assemble the burgers.
- For the burgers: When ready to cook, set the temperature to 350°F and preheat, lid closed for 15 minutes.
- Form into 5 equal patties and season both sides with Traeger Beef Rub.
- Place patties directly on the grill grate and cook for 4-5 minutes per side, flipping once. Top each burger with cheese and cook for 1 minute more to melt.
- Remove from the grill and let rest 1-2 minutes.
- To build burger, place the patty on the bottom bun, add a scoop of chili, Fritos, red onion and finish with the top bun. Enjoy

3.8 Traeger Filet Mignon
Ingredients:

- 3 Filet Mignon Steaks
- 1 Tsp Salt
- 1 Tsp Pepper
- 2 Cloves Garlic, Minced
- 3 Tbsp Butter, Softened

Instructions:

- In a small bowl combine salt, pepper, garlic, and softened butter. Rub on both sides of filets. Let rest 10 minutes.
- When ready to cook, set the temperature to 450°F and preheat, lid closed for 15 minutes.
- Place steaks directly on the grill and cook for 5-8 minutes on each side, or until the filets reach an internal temperature of 135-140 degrees F for medium rare. Enjoy!

3.9 Whiskey Bourbon BBQ Cheeseburger
Ingredients:

- 3 Lbs. Ground Beef
- 1/2 Cup Brown Sugar
- Hot Sauce to Taste
- 1/2 Cup Whiskey Bourbon
- Traeger Rub as Needed
- 1 Lb. Bacon
- 4 Slices Cheddar Cheese
- 1 Red Onion, Sliced
- 4 Large Hamburger Buns

Instructions:

- In a medium bowl, combine ground beef and Traeger Rub and mix well using caution not to overwork or allow the beef to get too warm.
- Divide the ground beef in quarters and put each quarter in a 6" cake ring. Press down and form the beef into a patty.
- With a skewer, poke about 40 holes about ¾" of the way through each patty. Spread brown sugar all over the top of the patties then drizzle with hot sauce. Pour whisky over each burger, transfer to the fridge and let sit for about a half hour.
- When ready to cook, set temperature to 225°F and preheat, lid closed for 10-15 minutes.
- Remove burgers from the cake rings. When the grill is to temp, place bacon and burgers directly on the grill grate and cook until burgers internal temperature reaches 165 °F. In the last ten minutes of cooking, top with cheddar cheese to melt.
- Remove burgers and bacon from the grill and build your burger to your liking. Enjoy!

3.10 Steak Taco Salad
Ingredients:

- 1 Avocado
- 1 Jalapeno
- 1 Egg Yolk
- 1/2 Bunch Cilantro
- 1 Clove Garlic
- Juice Of 1 Lime
- 1 Cup Canola Oil

Salad

- 2- 8 Oz Snake River Farm Top Sirloin Steaks
- Traeger Coffee Rub as Needed
- 1 Ear of Corn Shucked
- 1/2 Tbsp Olive Oil
- Salt to Taste
- 2 Hearts Romaine
- 1 Can Black Beans, Drained and Rinsed
- 1/4 Cup Pico De Gallo
- 1 Jalapeno, Thinly Sliced
- 1 Tbsp Cilantro Leaves, Torn

Instructions:

- When ready to cook, set temperature to 180°F and preheat, lid closed for 15 minutes. For optimal flavor, use Super Smoke if available.
- Cut the avocado in half and place it cut side up, directly on the grill grate. Smoke for 15-20 minutes until desired smoke flavor is achieved. Remove from grill and set aside to cool.
- Scoop the flesh from the smoked avocado and place in the pitcher of a blender. Add remaining **Ingredients:** except for the oil and puree until smooth. With the motor running, gradually add the oil a little bit at a time until it has all been added and the mixture is emulsified. Season with salt and lime juice to taste.

FOR THE SALAD:

- Season the steaks with Traeger coffee rub as needed. Brush the corn cob with olive oil and season with kosher salt.
- When ready to cook set the temperature to 450 °F and preheat lid closed for 10-15 minutes.
- Place the steaks and corn next to each other on the grill. Cook the steaks for about 5-7 minutes per side or until the internal temperature registers 130 °F for medium rare. Remove from grill and set aside to rest. Allow the corn to cook for 15-20 minutes until the kernels are tender and the exterior is golden brown. This will take longer than the steaks to cook but should be done by the time the steaks have finished resting.
- Chop the lettuce into bite sized pieces and place in a serving bowl. Toss with as much dressing as desired. Cut the kernels from the cob and sprinkle over the top of the dressed salad. Add black beans, Pico, jalapeno, cilantro.
- Thinly slice the steak and place on top of the salad. This salad, as is, is gluten free and dairy free but top with cheese if desired. Enjoy!

3.11 Cowboy Cut Steak
Ingredients:

- 2 Ea. Snake River Farms Cowboy Cut Steak (2.5 Lbs. Each)
- Traeger Beef Rub to Taste
- Kosher Salt
- Gremolata
- 1 Bunch Parsley
- 2 Tbsp Chopped Mint
- 1 Tbsp Preserved Lemon, Minced
- 1 Clove Garlic Minced
- 1/4 Cup Olive Oil
- Juice Of 1 Lemon
- Salt and Pepper to Taste

Instructions:

- Season the steaks liberally with Traeger Beef rub and kosher salt.
- When ready to cook, set the temperature to 225 °F (with Super Smoke if using a WiFIRE enabled grill) and preheat lid closed for 10-15 minutes.
- Place steaks directly on the grill grate and cook for 45 minutes or until the internal temperature reaches 115°F.
- Remove steaks from the grill and let rest for 10 minutes.
- While the steaks are resting, increase the grill temperature to high (450-500 °F) and preheat, lid closed for 10-15 minutes.
- Place the steaks back on the grill and cook 5-7 minutes per side or until the internal reaches 130 °F for medium rare.
- For the gremolata:
- In a medium bowl combine all **Ingredients:** and stir well. Adjust seasoning to taste with salt and lemon juice.
- Remove from the grill and let rest 1 minutes before slicing. Spoon gremolata over sliced steak to serve. Enjoy!

3.12 Grilled Butter Basted Porterhouse Steak
Ingredients:

- 4 Tbsp Butter, Melted
- 2 Tbsp Worcestershire Sauce
- 2 Tsp Dijon Mustard
- 2 Porterhouse Steaks (16-20 Oz And At Least 1-1/2" Thick)
- Traeger Prime Rib Rub

Instructions:

- When ready to cook, set the temperature to 225°F and preheat, lid closed for 15 minutes.
- Combine the melted butter, Worcestershire sauce, and mustard and whisk until smooth. Brush on both sides of the steaks with a pastry brush. Season the steaks on both sides with Traeger Prime Rib Rub.
- When grill is to temperature, arrange the steaks on the grill grate and cook for 30 minutes.
- With tongs, transfer the steaks to a platter and increase the heat to 450°F
- When grill reaches 450°F, return the steaks to the grill grate and grill until your desired degree of doneness. 140 degrees F for medium-rare, about 2-3 minutes on each side.
- Baste with the butter Worcestershire sauce mixture once more if desired.Let rest for 3 minutes before serving. Enjoy!

3.13 Tin Foil Dinner
Ingredients:

- 8 Tbsp Butter, Cut into Cubes
- 4 Sprigs Thyme
- 1 Garlic Clove, Minced
- 2 Green Bell Pepper, Chopped
- 1 Sm. Red Onion, Chopped
- 2 Whole Russet Potatoes, Peeled and Chopped
- 1 Lb. Stew Meat
- 1 Tsp Fish Sauce
- 1 Tbsp Worcestershire Sauce
- 1 Tbsp Traeger Veggie Rub
- Salt and Pepper

Instructions:

- When ready to cook, set the temperature to 350°F and preheat, lid closed for 15 minutes.
- Peel and chop potatoes into cubes. Peel and chop onions, peppers, and garlic.
- Place the stew meat in a medium bowl. Add the fish sauce and Worcestershire Sauce and mix well. Season with salt, pepper and Traeger Veggie Rub. Mix again to distribute evenly.
- Tear 4 pieces of foil and lay on a flat surface. Divide the potatoes evenly between the four sheets of foil then follow with onion, bell pepper, garlic and the stew meat- top off with thyme. Top each packet with 2 TBSP of butter.
- Fold the foil up and wrap tightly.
- Place the packets on a sheet tray and transfer to the grill. Cook for 45 minutes to one hour or until potatoes are cooked through and stew meat is tender.
- Remove from the grill, open up the packet and top with fresh herbs if desired. Enjoy!

3.14 Roasted Hatch Chile Burger with Smoked Cheese Sauce
Ingredients:

- Smoked Cheese Sauce
- 16 Oz Velveeta Cheese
- 2 Cloves Garlic, Minced
- 1 Tbsp Butter
- 1 Tsp Franks Red Hot
- 1/4 Cup Milk
- Burgers
- 1 Tbsp Butter
- 1/2 Yellow Onion, Thinly Sliced
- 2 Cloves Garlic, Minced
- 1 Lb. Roasted Hatch Green Chiles, Peeled Deseeded, Cut into Strips
- 2 Lbs. Ground Beef
- 3 Tsp Traeger Beef Rub
- 4 Ea. Burger Buns

Instructions:

- When ready to cook, set temperature to 180°F and preheat, lid closed for 15 minutes.
- For the Smoked Cheese Sauce: Heat 1 Tbsp butter in a small oven safe pan over medium-high heat. Add minced garlic and sauté 30 seconds. Add Velveeta cheese and stir until melted then add hot sauce.
- Transfer the pan to the grill and smoke for 30 minutes. Remove from heat and set aside until ready to use.
- For the Chile-Onions: Heat 1 Tbsp butter in a sauté pan over medium heat. Add onion and cook until translucent and tender, about 5-7 minutes. Add garlic and roasted chiles and cook until chiles are warmed through. Remove from heat and set aside until the burgers are finished.
- Increase the grill temperature to High. For optimal results, set to 500 degrees F if available.
- For the burgers: Form ground beef into 4 equal patties and season with Traeger Beef Rub.
- Place directly on the grill grate and cook for 8-10 minutes, flipping once halfway through.
- Cut burger buns in half and place directly on the grill grate. Toast buns for 2-3 minutes. To build the burgers, place the patty on the bottom bun, pour smoked cheese sauce on top and finish with hatch chile onion mixture. Enjoy!

3.15 Grilled Tomahawk Steak
Ingredients:

- 2 Large Tomahawk Steaks
- 2 Tbsp Kosher Salt
- 2 Tbsp Ground Black Pepper
- 1 Tbsp Paprika
- 1/2 Tbsp Garlic Powder
- 1/2 Tbsp Onion Powder
- 1/2 Tbsp Brown Sugar
- 1 Tsp Ground Mustard
- 1/4 Tsp Cayenne Pepper

Instructions:

- In a small bowl, combine all **Ingredients:** for the rub. Season the steaks liberally with the rub and set steaks aside while the grill preheats.
- When ready to cook, set temperature to 225°F and preheat, lid closed for 15 minutes. For optimal flavor, use Super Smoke if available.
- Place the steaks directly on the grill grate and smoke for 45 minutes to 1 hour, until the internal temperature reaches 120°F.
- Remove from the grill and set aside to rest.
- Increase the grill temperature to 450°F.
- Place the steaks directly on the grill grate and cook 7-10 minutes per side, or until the internal temperature reaches 130°F.
- Remove from grill and let rest 5 minutes before serving. Enjoy!

3.16 Smoked Chili Rib Eye Steaks
Ingredients:

- 4 Rib Eye Steaks, 10-12 Oz Each
- 2 Large Garlic Cloves, Minced
- 1 Tsp Salt
- 2 Tbsp Chili Powder
- 2 Tbsp Worcestershire Sauce
- 2 Tbsp Olive Oil
- 1 Tsp Packed Brown Sugar
- 1 Tsp Ground Cumin

Instructions:

- Mash the garlic and salt into a paste in a small bowl; stir in the chili powder, Worcestershire sauce, olive oil, brown sugar and cumin. Rub all surfaces of the steaks with the mixture.
- Place the steaks and the remaining rub into a large resealable plastic bag and refrigerate for 4 hours or up to 2 days.
- When ready to cook, set the temperature to 225°F and preheat, lid closed for 15 minutes.
- Place the steaks on the grill grate and smoke for about 45 minutes (until the internal temperature reaches 120°F).
- Remove the steaks and set aside to rest. Increase the temperature to High and preheat, lid closed for 10-15 minutes.
- Return the steaks to the grill and cook until your desired doneness. We love a good medium-rare, which is about 135 to 140°F, or about 3 to 5 minutes on the first side and a minute or two on the second side.
- Let the steaks rest for 5 to 10 minutes before serving. Enjoy!

3.17 Smoked Bourbon Jerky
Ingredients:

- 1 (3 Lb.) Flank Steak
- 1 Cup Bourbon
- 1/2 Cup Brown Sugar
- 1/4 Cup Traeger Jerky Rub
- 1 Can Chipotle End Adobo
- 3 Tbsp Worcestershire Sauce
- 1/2 Cup Apple Cider Vinegar

Instructions:

- Roll flank steak up parallel to the grain. Slice, going with the grain, into 1/4" thick slices.
- Combine all **Ingredients:** for marinade in a medium bowl and mix well.
- Place sliced flank steak into a large Ziploc bag and pour marinade over steak. Place in refrigerator and marinate overnight.
- When ready to cook, set temperature to 180°F and preheat, lid closed for 15 minutes.
- Remove flank from the marinade and place on a jerky rack or directly on the grill grate.
- Smoke for about 6 hours or until steak has dried out but is still pliable. Remove from grill and let cool at room temperature, lightly covered for 60 minutes before eating.
- Store in an airtight container or Ziploc bag in the refrigerator. Enjoy!

3.18 Slow Roasted Shawarma
Ingredients:

- 5.5 Lbs. Top Sirloin
- 5.5 Lbs. Boneless Skinless Chicken Thighs
- 4.5 Lbs. Lamb Fat
- 4 Tbsp Traeger Rub
- 2 Large Yellow Onions
- Pita Bread
- Topping Options: Cucumber, Tomatoes, Tahini, Pickles, Fries, Israeli Salad
- A Double Skewer
- A Cast Iron Griddle

Instructions:

- *Plan ahead! Assemble the shawarma stack the night before you plan to cook it.
- Slice all the meat and fat into ½" slices and place into 3 bowls (pro tip: it's easier to slice if they are all partially frozen).
- Season each bowl with Traeger Rub and massage the rub into the meat.
- Place half an onion on the bottom of each half skewer to make a firm base. then add 2 layers from each bowl at a time. Try to make the stack symmetrical, more or less. Then put the other 2 half onions at the top. Wrap in plastic wrap and refrigerate overnight.
- When ready to cook, set temperature to 275°F and preheat, lid closed for 15 minutes.
- Lay the shawarma directly on the grill grate and cook for about 3-4 hours, rotating at least once.
- Remove from grill and increase the temperature to 445°F. While the grill preheats, place a cast iron griddle directly on the grill grate and brush with olive oil.
- When the griddle is hot place the whole shawarma on the cast iron and sear 5-10 minutes per side. Remove from grill, slice off the edges, then repeat with remaining shawarma.
- Serve in pita bread with your favorite toppings like cucumber, tomatoes, tahini, pickles, fries or Israeli salad.
- Enjoy!

3.19 Reverse Seared Rib Eye Caps
Ingredients:

- 1 1/2 Lb. Rib Eye Cap
- 2 Tbsp Traeger Coffee Rub
- 2 Tbsp Traeger Beef Rub

Instructions:

- Trim the Rib Eye Cap of excess silver skin and fat, if needed. Cut the cap into 4 equal portions and roll into steaks. Tie with butchers' twine to secure.
- In a small bowl, combine both rubs. Season the steaks liberally with the rub mixture and set aside while the grill heats up.
- When ready to cook, set temperature to 225°F and preheat, lid closed for 15 minutes. For optimal flavor, use Super Smoke if available.
- Place the steaks directly on the grill grate, and smoke for 30-45 minutes until the internal temperature reaches 120°F.
- Remove from the grill and set aside to rest.
- Increase the grill temperature to 450°F.
- Place the steaks directly on the grill grate and cook 3-4 minutes per side, or until the internal temperature reaches 130°F.
- Remove from grill and let rest 5 minutes before serving.
- Enjoy!

3.20 BBQ Beef Short Ribs
Ingredients:

- 4 Ea. (4 Bone) Beef Short Rib Racks
- 1/2 Cup Traeger Beef Rub
- 1 Cup Apple Juice

Instructions:

- If your butcher has not already done so, remove the thin papery membrane from the bone-side of the ribs by working the tip of a butter knife underneath the membrane over a middle bone. Use paper towels to get a firm grip, then tear the membrane off.
- Season both sides of ribs with Traeger Beef Rub.
- When ready to cook, set the Traeger to 225°F and preheat, lid closed for 15 minutes.
- Arrange the ribs on the grill grate, bone side down.
- Cook for 8-10 hours, spritzing or mopping with apple juice every 60 minutes until internal temperature reaches 205°F.
- Slice between ribs and serve immediately. Enjoy!

3.21 Grilled T-Bone Steaks with Bloody Mary Steak Sauce
Ingredients:

- 2 Large T-Bone Steaks
- 1 Tbsp Kosher Salt
- 1 Tbsp Black Pepper
- 1 Cup Smoked Bloody Mary Mix
- 1/2 White Onion, Small Dice
- 1 Clove Garlic, Minced
- Juice Of 1 Lemon
- 1 Tbsp Soy Sauce
- 2 Tbsp Brown Sugar
- 1 Tbsp Mustard
- 2 Tbsp Olive Oil

Instructions:

- When ready to cook, set temperature to 225°F and preheat, lid closed for 15 minutes. For optimal flavor, use Super Smoke if available.
- Season the steaks with salt and pepper and place directly on the grill grate and smoke for 60-90 minutes until the internal temperature reaches 125°F when an instant read thermometer is inserted into the thickest part of the steak.
- For the Steak Sauce: Place olive oil in a medium sauce pan over medium heat. Add onion and garlic and sauté 5 minutes until the onions are lightly browned and translucent. Add remaining **Ingredients:** and reduce the heat to a simmer. Simmer for 20-30 minutes until the mixture has reduced and thickened.
- Remove the steaks from the grill and increase the temperature to High.
- When the grill is hot, sear the stakes for 5 minutes on each side. Remove from the grill and let rest 10 minutes before serving.
- Serve steak with steak sauce on the side warm or room temperature. Enjoy

3.22 Grilled Thai Beef Salad
Ingredients:

- 1.5 Lb. Hanger or Skirt Steak
- Salt, To Taste
- Cracked White Pepper, To Taste
- 2-4 (Depending on Spice Preference) Fresh Hot Thai Chili Peppers (Or Jalapeños), Minced Very Thin
- 1 Garlic Clove, Chopped and Minced Fine
- 4 Tbsp Thai Fish Sauce
- 4 Tbsp Fresh Squeezed Lime Juice
- 1 Tbsp Toasted Sticky Rice Powder (Optional)
- 1 Tbsp Palm or Brown Sugar
- 1 Heart of Romaine Lettuce, Chopped
- 1 English Cucumber Without Seeds, Sliced Thin on A Bias Cut
- 1 Handful Fresh Mint Leaves, Roughly Chopped
- 6 Cherry Tomatoes, Halved
- 1 Small Red Onion, Sliced Very Thin
- 2 Green Onions Cut Into 1/4" Pieces
- 2 Sprigs Cilantro Without Stems, Roughly Chopped

Instructions:

- When ready to cook, set temperature to High and preheat, lid closed for 15 minutes.
- Season both sides of steak with salt and cracked white pepper. Brush the grill with canola oil to prevent steaks from sticking.
- Grill hanger steak until it reaches an internal temperature of 130°F for medium rare, about 5-10 minutes. Allow meat to rest then slice thin.
- For the Dressing: Mix together the garlic, chili peppers, fish sauce, lime juice and sugar in a small bowl. Add the toasted rice powder last. Note: If toasted rice powder is not accessible, use uncooked rice and dry roast in a pan over low heat until golden brown and grind into a powder with a mortar and pestle or food processor to add a nutty texture.
- Add the sliced hanger steak to the dressing and toss well.

- In another bowl, add all the herbs with the chopped romaine cucumbers and tomatoes and toss everything together with the dressing and the hanger steak.
- Add additional fish sauce, lime juice, sugar, toasted rice powder and chili peppers based on your taste preference.
- Garnish with cilantro and mint. Enjoy!

3.23 Grilled Ribeye with Green Butter
Ingredients:

- Ribeye Steak
- 3 Ribeye Steaks, 1 1/2-2" Thickness
- 1/4 Cup Kosher Salt
- 1/4 Cup Coarse Ground Black Pepper
- 3 Tbsp Onion Powder
- Green Butter
- 1 Stick Butter, Room Temperature
- 1 1/2 Tbsp Flat Leaf Parsley, Chopped
- 1/2 Tsp Garlic, Minced
- Pinch White Pepper
- Juice Of 1/2 Lemon

Instructions:

- When ready to cook, set the Traeger to 225°F and preheat, lid closed for 15 minutes.
- For the Green Butter: Combine all **Ingredients:** for the green butter and place in the fridge until ready to use.
- Combine the salt, pepper and onion powder. Rub the mixture on the steaks and place them on the grill.
- Cook until steaks reach an internal temperature of 120°F. This should take approximately 75-90 minutes.
- Remove steaks from the grill and tent with foil. Increase the grill temperature to High and let it come to temperature.
- When the grill is hot, place the steaks back on the grill for 4 minutes per side, adding a tablespoon of the green butter after the first flip.
- Top with green butter if desired. Enjoy!

3.24 Smoked Peppered Beef Tenderloin
Ingredients:

- 1(2-2 1/2 Lb.) Snake River Farms Beef Tenderloin Roast, Trimmed
- 1/2 Cup Dijon Mustard
- 2 Cloves Garlic, Minced to A Paste
- 2 Tbsp Bourbon or Strong Cold Coffee
- Jacobsen Salt, As Needed
- Coarsely Ground Black and Green Peppercorns, As Needed

Instructions:

- Lay the tenderloin on a large piece of plastic wrap.
- Combine the mustard, garlic, and bourbon in a small bowl. Slather the mixture evenly all over the tenderloin. Allow to sit at room temperature for 1 hour.
- Unwrap the plastic wrap and generously season the tenderloin on all sides with the salt and ground black and green peppercorns.
- When ready to cook, set temperature to 180°F and preheat, lid closed for 15 minutes.
- Arrange the tenderloin directly on the grill grate and smoke for 60 minutes.
- Increase the grill temperature to 400°F and roast the tenderloin until the internal temperature reaches 130°F, about 20 to 30 minutes depending on the thickness of the tenderloin. Do not overcook.
- Let rest for 10 minutes before slicing. Enjoy!

3.25 BBQ Sweet Pepper Meatloaf
Ingredients:

- 5 Lb. 80/20 Ground Beef
- 2 Eggs
- 1 Cup Plain Panko Bread Crumbs
- 1 Tbsp Kosher Salt
- 1 Tbsp Black Pepper
- 2 Tbsp Traeger Rub
- 1 Cup Finely Chopped Red Sweet Peppers
- 1 Cup Finely Chopped Green Onion
- 1 Cup Ketchup

Instructions:

- Thoroughly mix together the ground beef, eggs, plain panko bread crumbs, kosher salt, black pepper, Traeger rub, red sweet peppers and green onion.
- When ready to cook, set the temperature to 225°F and preheat, lid closed for 15 minutes.
- Mold the meat mixture into a loaf and season exterior with the Traeger rub.
- Place meatloaf directly on the grill grate and cook for 2 hours and 15 minutes.
- Increase the grill temperature to 375°F and cook until an internal temperature of 155°F.
- Glaze the meatloaf with ketchup and cook an additional 15 minutes.
- Allow to rest for 15 minutes before slicing. Enjoy!

3.26 Traeger Pot Roast Sandwich
Ingredients:

- Pot Roast
- 1 (3-4 Lb.) Chuck Roast
- Traeger Beef Rub, As Needed
- 2 Qtrs. Beef Stock
- 1 Carrot, Peeled and Chopped into Chunks
- 1 Stalk Celery, Chopped into Chunks
- 1 Small Yellow Onion, Peeled and Cut into Chunks
- 4 Cloves Garlic
- 2 Tbsp Cumin
- 2 Tbsp Chili Powder
- 2 Tbsp Garlic Powder
- 2 Tbsp Onion Powder
- 6 Slices Provolone
- 2 Loafs Crusty Bread, Such as Baguette or Sourdough
- Leek Marmalade
- 1/2 Cup 3 Leeks, Thinly Sliced, Washed and Dried
- 1/4 Cup Butter
- 1 Tbsp Yellow or Brown Mustard Seeds
- 1/4 Cup Sherry Vinegar
- 1/4 Cup Brown Sugar
- Salt, To Taste
- Horseradish Mayonnaise
- 1/2 Cup Mayonnaise
- Prepared Horseradish, To Taste

Instructions:

- When ready to cook, set the temperature to 400°F and preheat, lid closed for 15 minutes.
- Season the roast liberally with Traeger Beef rub and place on directly on the grill grate. Roast for 20-30 minutes until the outside is caramelized.
- Remove roast from the grill and place in a large pot. Reduce the grill temperature to 325°F.
- Add beef stock (the liquid should cover about 3/4 the height of the roast) and add carrot, celery, onion and spices. Stir to distribute evenly making sure there are no vegetables on top of the roast.
- Cover the pot and place back on the grill. Braise for 3-4 hours until the roast is fork tender.
- Remove the roast from the braising liquid and shred, discarding any large pieces of fat or sinew.
- For the Gravy: Strain the liquid and place back in the pot. Bring the liquid to a boil then reduce to a simmer. Thicken the liquid with cornstarch to desired consistency.
- Pour a bit of the gravy over the reserved shredded meat and reserve the rest to dip.
- Make sure leeks are washed well. The easiest way to do this is to slice the leeks, submerge them in a bucket of water and stir vigorously to remove the dirt. Lift the leeks out of the water into a strainer and shake off excess and dry.
- For the Leek Marmalade: Melt the butter in a medium sauce pan over medium high heat. Add leeks and reduce heat to medium. Cook the leeks stirring occasionally until completely softened and falling apart. Add the mustard seeds, vinegar and brown sugar and stir to combine. Simmer for 20-30 minutes until the liquid reduces and thickens. Season to taste with salt. Remove from heat and let cool.
- For the Horseradish Mayo: In a small bowl combine mayo and horseradish and set aside.
- Split loafs lengthwise and portion into 6-8 sandwiches.
- Spread a bit of the horseradish mayo and leek marmalade onto each half of the bread. Top each half with shredded beef and a slice of provolone.
- Place sandwich halves back on the grill (set at 325°F) long enough to melt the cheese, about 5 minutes.
- Remove from grill and serve open faced or with two halves together to make a sandwich. Serve with extra gravy to dip. Enjoy!

3.27 Grilled Steak Salad
Ingredients:

- 1 Ea. (1.5 Lb.) Black Flat Iron Steak
- Traeger Beef Rub
- 8 Oz Arugula
- 8 Oz Baby Spinach
- 1/4 Cup Cherry Tomatoes, Halved
- 1/2 Red Onion, Thinly Sliced
- 1/4 Cup Blue Cheese
- 2 Tbsp Balsamic Vinegar
- 4 Tbsp Extra Virgin Olive Oil
- Coarse Sea Salt and Fresh Black Pepper, To Taste

Instructions:

- When ready to cook, set temperature to High and preheat, lid closed for 15 minutes.
- Trim any sinew or silver skin from the flat iron steak. Season liberally with Traeger Beef rub and kosher salt.
- When the grill is hot, place steak directly on the grill grate. Cook for 10-15 minutes then flip and cook 10 minutes more. Remove from the grill when the internal temperature reaches 130°F when an instant read thermometer is inserted into the thickest part. Let steak rest 10 minutes before slicing.
- While the steak is resting, build the salad. In a large bowl combine the greens, tomatoes, onion and blue cheese. Drizzle with balsamic and olive oil and toss.
- Place salad on a large platter and top with sliced steak. Finish with a sprinkle of sea salt and fresh black pepper. Enjoy!

3.28 Smoked Corned Beef & Cabbage
Ingredients:

- 1 (3 To 5 Lb.) Corned Beef Brisket
- 1 Qtr. Chicken Stock
- 1 (12 Oz) Can Beer, Preferably A Pilsner or Lager
- 1/2 Cup (1 Stick) Butter, Cut into Slices
- 1/4 Tsp Garlic Salt
- 2 Tbsp Fresh Dill, Chopped
- 2 Cups Baby Carrots
- 1 Lb. Baby Potatoes or Fingerlings
- 1 Head Cabbage, Cut in Wedges

Instructions:

- When ready to cook, set the temperature to 180°F and preheat, lid closed for 15 minutes.
- Rinse brisket and pat dry. Place directly on the grill grate and smoke for 2 hours.
- Increase grill temperature to 325°F and preheat, lid closed.
- Remove brisket from grill and place in a roasting pan. Sprinkle seasoning packet on top. Pour chicken stock and dark beer over the roast and into the pan.
- Cover roasting pan with foil and place on the grill. Cook for 2 1/2 hours or until beef is fork tender.
- Remove foil and add carrots and potatoes to the roasting pan. Cover meat and vegetables with garlic salt and butter slices.
- Recover with foil and cook for an additional 20 minutes or until carrots and potatoes are just tender. Add cabbage, cover and return to grill for 20 minutes more.
- Remove vegetables from the pan to a bowl or serving platter. Slice beef and serve with potatoes, cabbage and carrots.
- Garnish with fresh dill and thyme if desired. Enjoy!

3.29 Traeger French Dip Sandwich
Ingredients:

- Roast Beef
- 1 (2-2.5 Lb.) Snake River Farms Manhattan Roast
- Traeger Beef Rub, As Needed
- Kosher Salt, As Needed
- Caramelized Onions
- 2 Yellow Onions, Thinly Sliced
- 1 Tbsp Butter
- Salt, To Taste
- Au Jus
- 1 Qtr. Good Quality Beef Stock
- 1 Sprig Thyme
- 1 Sprig Rosemary
- 4 Peppercorns
- 2 Cloves Garlic
- Sandwich
- 2 Baguettes Cut into Sandwich Sized Rolls, Or Hoagie Rolls
- Mayonnaise, As Needed
- 6 Slices Provolone Cheese

Instructions:

- When ready to cook, set the temperature to High and preheat, lid closed for 15 minutes.
- Season the roast liberally with Traeger Beef Rub and salt.
- Place roast directly on the grill grate and cook for 45 minutes until the exterior starts to caramelize and brown.
- Reduce the grill temperature to 325°F and continue to cook roast until the internal temperature reaches 125°F, about 75 minutes.
- Remove roast from grill and let rest for 15 minutes before slicing.
- After resting, thinly slice the meat on a meat slicer or with a very sharp knife. Set meat aside.
- For the Caramelized Onions: Place butter and onions in a sauté pan and cook over medium heat. Season liberally with salt and cook, stirring frequently until the onions are browned and caramelized. If the bottom of the pan starts to stick before

the onions are completely cooked through, add 1 Tbsp of water, scrape up the browned bits with a wooden spoon and continue to cook. When completely softened and caramelized, remove from the heat and set aside until ready to build the sandwiches.

- For the Au Jus: Place the **Ingredients:** for the au jus in a pot and bring to a simmer. Cook for 30-45 minutes, season liberally with salt and strain the solids out.
- Toast the buns cut side down on the grill for 5-10 minutes until lightly browned.
- To build the sandwiches, place them toasted side up on a sheet tray. Spread the mayonnaise on the bun, top with the thinly sliced meat, then caramelized onions and cheese.
- Place the tray directly on the grill grate and cook just until the cheese is melted.
- Serve sandwiches hot with au jus. Enjoy!

3.30 3-2-1 BBQ Beef Cheek
Ingredients:

- 2 Ea. (About 2 Lb.) Beef Cheeks, Trimmed of Silver skin
- Traeger Beef Rub, As Needed
- 1/4 Cup Liquid of Your Choice (Beef Stock, Dark Beer Etc)
- 2 Tbsp Honey, Brown Sugar, Or Other Sweetener

Instructions:

- Make sure the beef cheeks are trimmed of all silver skin. Season liberally with Traeger Beef rub.
- When ready to cook, set temperature to 180°F and preheat, lid closed for 15 minutes.
- Place beef cheeks directly on the grill grate and cook until they reach an internal temperature of 165°F, about 3 hours. Remove from grill and place the cheeks in a small rimmed baking dish.
- Increase grill temperature to 225°F.
- In a small bowl, combine liquid and sweetener and stir until sweetener is dissolved. Pour mixture into the baking dish and return the cheeks to the grill to cook for an additional two hours.
- Remove cheeks from the grill and cover with foil. Return to the grill to cook for an additional hour or until the internal temperature reaches 205°F.
- Remove from the grill and allow the steam to escape. Wrap with foil again and let rest for 30 minutes before shredding or slicing. Enjoy!

3.31 Grilled Wagyu Burgers
Ingredients:

- 2 Lb. Snake River Farms Wagyu Ground Beef
- Salt and Pepper, To Taste
- Burger Buns
- Butter Lettuce
- Heirloom Tomatoes, Sliced
- Red Onion, Sliced
- American Cheese

Instructions:

- When ready to cook, set the temperature to High and preheat, lid closed for 15 minutes.
- Form six burger patties and season liberally with salt and pepper.
- When the grill is hot, place burger patties directly on the grill grate and cook for 4 minutes.
- Flip the burgers, top with cheese and cook for 4 minutes longer.
- Remove from grill and let rest 2 minutes.
- Build your burger and top with desired condiments. Enjoy!

3.32 Braised Italian Meatballs
Ingredients:

- 1 Lb. Ground Beef
- 1 Lb. Ground Pork
- 4 Oz Prosciutto, Finely Diced
- 1 Cup Fresh Bread Crumbs
- Kosher Salt
- 2 Tsp Fennel Seeds
- 1 Tsp Oregano
- 1 Cup Whole-Milk Ricotta Cheese
- 1/2 Cup Milk
- 3 Eggs, Whisked
- 1 (28 Oz) Can Crushed Tomatoes, In Their Juices
- Extra-Virgin Olive Oil
- 1/2 Cup Basil Leaves

Instructions:

- When ready to cook, set the temperature to 375°F and preheat, lid closed for 15 minutes.
- In a large mixing bowl, combine the ground beef, pork, prosciutto, bread crumbs, 2 tsp salt, fennel seed, and oregano.
- In a separate mixing bowl, combine the ricotta, milk, and eggs and whisk to combine.
- Using freshly washed hands, combine the meats with the bread crumbs, salt, and herbs until the mixture is evenly combined and the herbs are evenly incorporated.
- Slowly pour the liquid mixture over the meat and continue to use your hands to combine. The mixture will be tacky even when well mixed. Allow to sit for 10 minutes.
- Pro Tip: To check the seasoning of your mixture before cooking off the entire batch, form 1 2-inch patty and cook in a small sauté pan until cooked through, about 2 minutes per side. Taste and adjust the seasoning of the meat mixture as needed.
- Line a large baking sheet with parchment or Traeger butcher paper. Alternately, lightly grease the baking sheet.
- Using clean hands or an ice cream scoop, form meatballs into the size of golf balls.
- Arrange them on the baking sheet with a little space between each so they are not touching. The mixture should yield about 48 meatballs.
- Place the baking sheet directly on the grill and cook, turning the meatballs once, until cooked through when cut in half, about 20 minutes.
- Remove from the grill, add the second batch if necessary, and repeat.
- Reduce the grill temperature to 300°F.
- When the meatballs are cool enough to handle, place all of them in a large roasting pan. Pour the crushed tomatoes over the top. Sprinkle with an additional teaspoon of salt and drizzle 3 tbsp of olive oil over the top.
- Cover the pan tightly with aluminum foil. Place on the grill and cook, covered, for 60-90 minutes or until the tomatoes have absorbed some of the flavor from the meatballs and the meatballs are fork tender.
- Remove meatballs from the grill and sprinkle with basil. Alternately, the meatballs can be roasted, cooled, and refrigerated a day in advance, then brought to room temperature and braised in the tomato sauce before serving. Enjoy!

3.33 Grilled Piranha
Ingredients:

- 1 (2.5 Lb.) Snake River Farms Wagyu Piranha
- Kosher Salt

Instructions:

- Cut the piranha into steaks about 1-inch thick. Fold them in half to form a "C" shape with the fat cap on the outer edge.
- Thread the steaks onto a skewer one on top of the other. Season generously with coarse salt and leave at room temperature while the grill heats up.
- When ready to cook, set the temperature to High and preheat, lid closed for 15 minutes.
- Place the skewered steaks directly on the grill grate and cook for 5-7 minutes per side or until desired internal temperature is reached, 130°F for medium-rare.
- Let rest 5 minutes before slicing. Enjoy!

3.34 Reverse Seared Porterhouse Steak
Ingredients:

- 1-2 (About 2 Lb.) Dry Aged Porterhouse Steaks
- Kosher Salt
- 8 Cups Arugula
- Extra-Virgin Olive Oil
- Freshly Ground Pepper
- 3 Oz Parmigiano-Reggiano

Instructions:

- Two hours before cooking, remove the steaks from the refrigerator and allow to come to room temperature. Pat dry with a paper towel.
- When ready to cook, set temperature to 225°F and preheat, lid closed for 15 minutes. For optimal flavor, use Super Smoke if available.
- Season both sides of steak with a generous amount of salt. Place steaks on grill and cook for 30 to 45 minutes or until an instant read thermometer inserted in the thickest part of the meat reads 120°F.
- Remove steaks from grill and turn the grill temperature up to High. For optimal results, set to 500°F if available.
- Place the steaks back on grill and sear on both sides for 3 minutes or until desired internal temperature is reached, 125-130°F for medium rare. Remove from grill and let rest 10 minutes before slicing. Slice the meat against the grain into 1/2" thick slices.
- To serve, place the arugula on a large platter. Drizzle arugula with olive oil and sprinkle with salt. Place the sliced steak and its juices on top of the arugula.
- Add a fresh grinding of pepper over the steak and shave the Parmigiano-Reggiano over the top of the steak. Enjoy!

3.35 Reverse Seared Filet Mignon with Red Wine Reduction
Ingredients:

- Bacon Wrapped Filet Mignon
- 2 Ea. Filet Mignon
- 2 Slices Bacon
- Traeger Prime Rib Rub, As Needed
- Toothpicks
- Red Wine Reduction
- 1 Tbsp Butter
- 1 Shallot, Thinly Sliced
- 1/2 Cup Red Wine
- 1/2 Cup Beef Stock
- 1 Tsp Chopped Rosemary
- 1 Tbsp Cold Butter
- Salt, To Taste

Instructions:

- When ready to cook, set the temperature to 225°F and preheat, lid closed for 15 minutes.
- Wrap each filet with a slice of bacon and secure with a tooth pick. Season liberally with Traeger Prime Rib rub.
- Place steaks directly on the grill grate and cook until the internal temperature reaches 115°F, start checking after about 20 minutes.
- Remove steaks from grill and set aside. Increase grill temperature to High and let preheat 10 minutes.
- For the Red-Wine Reduction Sauce: In a sauté pan over medium heat, melt 1 Tbsp butter and shallots and sauté until translucent. Add red wine and beef stock and bring to a simmer. Reduce the heat and let simmer until reduced by half. Add rosemary, remove from heat and whisk in the 1 Tbsp cold butter. Season with salt to taste.
- When grill is hot, place steaks back on the grill and sear for 5-7 minutes on each side or until the internal temperature reaches 125°F for medium-rare.
- Remove from grill and let rest 5-7 minutes before serving.
- Serve steaks with your favorite sides and spoonful of red wine reduction sauce over the top. Enjoy!

3.36 Grilled Flank Steak with Peperomia
Ingredients:

- Flank Steak
- 1/4 Cup Olive Oil
- 2 Tbsp Red Wine Vinegar
- 2 Tbsp Brown Sugar
- 2 Tsp Salt
- 1 Tsp Fennel Seeds
- 1 Tsp Paprika
- 1/2 Tsp Freshly Ground Black Pepper
- 2 Cloves Garlic, Crushed
- 1 (2 Lb.) Flank Steak
- Peperomia
- 5 Red or Yellow Bell Peppers (Combination Preferred)
- 1/4 Cup Extra-Virgin Olive Oil, Plus More for Finishing
- Kosher Salt
- 1 Yellow Onion, Thinly Sliced
- 2 Small Fennel Bulbs, Core and Stems Removed, Thinly Sliced
- 2 Cloves Garlic, Peeled and Minced
- 1/4 Tsp Crushed Red Pepper Flakes
- 2 Tbsp Capers, Rinsed and Drained
- 2 Tbsp Sherry Vinegar
- 1/4 Cup Thinly Sliced Basil

Instructions:

- For the Marinade: Combine the olive oil, vinegar, sugar, spices, and the garlic in a baking dish that is large enough to hold the flank steak. Stir to combine.
- Add the flank steak to marinade and turn to coat. Cover with plastic wrap and refrigerate for 1-8 hours. Remove the meat from the refrigerator one hour before grilling.
- For the peperomia, when ready to cook, set temperature to High and preheat, lid closed for 15 minutes.
- Line a baking sheet with aluminum foil.
- Place the bell peppers in a large bowl. Drizzle with 1 Tbsp of the olive oil, sprinkle with a teaspoon of salt and toss until the peppers are well coated. Transfer to the prepared baking sheet.
- Roast for 15 minutes on the grill, turn the peppers, and continue roasting until the peppers are charred and soft, with their skins beginning to peel away, an additional 20 minutes.
- Return the peppers to the large bowl, cover tightly with plastic wrap, and let sit for 10 minutes. When the peppers are cool enough to handle, remove the stems, skin, and seeds. Cut the flesh into rough strips and set aside.
- In a large saute pan over medium heat, warm the remaining 4 Tbsp olive oil. Add the onion and fennel and cook, stirring occasionally, until softened, about 8 to 10 minutes.
- Add the garlic, crushed red pepper, and ½ tsp salt and cook, stirring constantly, until fragrant, about 1 minutes. Stir in the capers and vinegar and allow the vinegar to reduce for 1 minute. Remove from the heat and stir in the roasted peppers.
- Taste and adjust the salt and pepper as desired. If using immediately, finish with a generous drizzle of extra-virgin olive oil.
- To grill the steak, set the temperature to High on the grill and preheat, lid closed for 15 minutes.
- Remove the steak from the marinade and pat dry with paper towels. Place on the grill and cook, turning once, until the internal temperature reaches 135 degrees for medium-rare, about 10 minutes per side.
- Remove from the grill and allow to rest for 10 minutes before slicing.
- Serve flank steak with the peperomia. Enjoy!

3.37 Grilled Cheesesteak Sandwich
Ingredients:

- 1.5 Lbs. Snake River Farms New York Strip Slices
- Traeger Beef Rub, As Needed
- Salt and Pepper, To Taste
- 1 Tbsp Canola Oil
- 1 Green Bell Pepper, Sliced
- 1 Yellow Bell Pepper, Sliced
- 1 Red Bell Pepper, Sliced
- 1 Large Yellow Onion, Sliced into Rounds
- Provolone Cheese
- Hoagie Rolls

Instructions:

- When ready to cook, set the temperature to High and preheat, lid closed for 15 minutes.
- Place a cast iron griddle directly on the grill grate while the grill preheats.
- Season the peppers and onions liberally with salt and pepper. Season the strip slices with Traeger Beef rub.
- Lightly oil the cast iron griddle with 1 Tbsp canola oil. Add onions and season with salt.
- Sauté 5 minutes until translucent. Add peppers and sauté 10 minutes more until peppers are softened and cooked through.
- While the peppers and onions are cooking, place the seasoned steak strips directly on the grill grate next to the griddle and cook for 3 minutes per side until lightly browned and cooked through.
- Place buns cut side down on the top grill grate to toast.
- When the steak is done, transfer to the griddle to build the sandwiches. Place a pile of peppers and onions on top of each pile of steak and top with a slice of provolone.
- Close the lid and let the cheese melt. Using two spatulas, transfer each pile to the buns and serve hot. Enjoy!

3.38 Reverse Seared Ny Strip Steak
Ingredients:

- 4 (1-1/2" Inch Thick) New York Strip Steaks
- Traeger Beef Rub
- 4 Tbsp Butter

Instructions:

- When ready to cook, set the Traeger to 225°F and preheat, lid closed for 15 minutes. For optimal flavor, use Super Smoke if available.
- While the grill is coming up to temperature, season the steaks with Traeger Beef rub.
- Place the steaks in the grill and smoke for 60 minutes or until they reach an internal temperature of 105 to 110°F. Remove steaks from grill and set on the counter to rest.
- Increase the grill temperature to 450°F. For optimal results, set to 500°F if available and let it come up to temperature with the lid close, about 10 minutes.
- Return steaks to grill and sear for 4 minutes. Flip steaks and add 1 tbsp butter to each steak.
- Sear for another 4 minutes and check the internal temperature. The desired finish temperature is 130 to 135°F for medium-rare.Once desired temperature is reached, remove steaks from grill. Let rest 5 minutes. Enjoy!

3.39 Traeger Ny Strip Steak
Ingredients:

- 1 (14 Oz) New York Strip Steak
- Traeger Beef Rub
- 1 Cup Traeger Sweet & Heat BBQ Sauce

Instructions:

- Pour the Sweet & Heat BBQ Sauce into a shallow casserole dish, stirring to combine.
- Place the strip steak in the mixture, making sure the steak is coated evenly on both sides. Cover with plastic wrap and marinate in the refrigerator for a minimum of 3 hours to overnight.
- Remove the steak from the marinade and season with Traeger Beef rub. Let steaks come to room temperature before grilling, about 45 minutes.
- When ready to cook, set temperature to High and preheat, lid closed for 15 minutes.
- Place steak toward the front of the grill grate and cook for 4-5 minutes on each side until steaks reach desired internal temperature, 130°F for medium-rare.
- Remove from the grill and let rest for 5 minutes. Slice against the grain to serve. Enjoy!

3.40 Grilled Peppercorn Steaks with Mushroom Cream Sauce
Ingredients:

- Peppercorn Steaks
- 4 Beef Steaks, Preferably Beef Tenderloin Steaks
- 1/2 Cup Dijon Mustard
- 2 Cloves Garlic, Minced to A Paste
- 2 Tbsp Bourbon or Strong Cold Coffee
- Kosher Salt
- Black Pepper and Green Peppercorns, Coarsely Ground
- Mushroom Cream Sauce
- 1 Tbsp Olive Oil
- 16 Oz Cremini Mushrooms, Thinly Sliced
- 1 Clove Garlic, Minced
- 1/2 Cup White Wine
- 1/2 Cup Chicken Stock
- 1/2 Cup Heavy Cream
- Salt and Pepper, To Taste

Instructions:

- In a small bowl, add the mustard, garlic, bourbon, and Worcestershire sauce. Whisk to combine.
- Lay the steaks on a large piece of plastic wrap and slather the mixture evenly all over the tenderloin. Bring the sides of the plastic wrap over the tenderloin and wrap tightly. Allow to sit at room temperature for 60 minutes.
- Unwrap the plastic wrap and generously season the tenderloin on all sides with salt, ground black pepper and green peppercorns. Use your hands to pat the peppercorns into the steak.
- When ready to cook, set temperature to 180°F and preheat, lid closed for 15 minutes. For optimal flavor, use Super Smoke if available.

- Arrange the steaks directly on the grill grate and smoke for 60 minutes. Remove the steaks from the grill.
- Increase the grill temperature to High allow the grill to preheat with the lid closed.
- When grill is hot, return the steaks to the grill and cook until the internal temperature reaches 130°F on an instant-read meat thermometer, about 20 to 30 minutes, depending on the thickness of the steak. Do not overcook.
- For the Mushroom Cream Sauce: Heat olive oil in a large sauté pan over medium heat. Add sliced onions, being careful not to crowd the pan and sauté until softened and lightly browned. Add garlic and sauté 1 minute more. Add the white wine and chicken stock to the mushrooms and bring to a simmer. Simmer for 5-7 minutes then reduce the heat and stir in the cream. Season to taste with salt and pepper. Remove from heat and set aside.
- Transfer steaks to a platter and cover with foil. Let rest for 10 minutes before removing the foil and carving into thin slices.
- To serve, spoon the sauce directly onto the steaks. Enjoy!

3.41 BBQ Brisket Grilled Chees
Ingredients:

- 4 Oz Leftover Brisket
- 2 Slices Texas Toast
- 2 Slices American Cheese
- 1 Tbsp Butter, Room Temperature

Instructions:

- When ready to cook, set the temperature to High and preheat, lid closed for 15 minutes.
- Place a skillet or griddle directly on the grill grate with the flat side up to preheat.
- Butter one side of each piece of bread. Place the buttered side of one piece down on the skillet or griddle, top with one slice of American cheese, the brisket, second slice of cheese, then the other piece of toast buttered side up.
- Close the grill lid and let cook for 5-7 minutes. Flip the sandwich and cook for 5 minutes more.
- Remove from the grill and slice in half. Enjoy!

3.42 Smoked Pastrami Sandwich
Ingredients:

- Brine
- 1 (4-5 Lbs.) Beef Brisket Flat, Fat Trimmed To 1/4-Inch
- 1 Gallon Water
- 6 Cloves Garlic, Peeled and Smashed
- 5 Juniper Berries
- 3 Bay Leaves, Broken into Pieces
- 3/4 Cup Kosher Salt
- 1/2 Cup Brown Sugar
- 2 Tbsp Morton's Tender quick Curing Salt (Optional)
- Rub
- 1 Tbsp Whole Black Peppercorns
- 3 Tbsp Coarsely Ground Black Pepper
- 3 Tbsp Coriander Seeds
- 1 Tbsp Yellow Mustard Seeds
- 2 Bay Leaves
- 1/4 Cup Brown Sugar
- 2 Tbsp Sweet Paprika
- 1 Tbsp Kosher Salt
- 1 Tsp Ground Cinnamon
- 1/2 Tsp Ground Clove
- Sandwich
- 1/2 Cup Mayonnaise
- 2 Tsp Dijon
- 2 Tsp Horseradish
- 1 Clove Garlic, Minced
- Salt and Pepper
- Rye Bread
- Swiss Cheese

Instructions:

- Plan ahead! This recipe requires brining for 3 days and refrigeration overnight.
- For the Brine: Bring the water to a boil in a large pot. Stir in the garlic, juniper berries, bay leaves, salt, brown sugar, curing salt, if using, whole peppercorns and allspice berries. Let cool completely, then immerse the meat weighing it down with a plate if necessary. Refrigerate for 3 days.
- For the Rub: In a spice grinder or small food processor, combine the black pepper, coriander seeds, mustard seeds, and bay leaves and pulse until coarsely ground. Stir in the brown sugar, paprika, cinnamon, and clove.
- Remove the meat from the brine and rinse under cold running water and pat dry with paper towels. Sprinkle the rub on the brisket and cover tightly with plastic wrap. Refrigerate for 24 hours.
- When ready to cook, set temperature to 225°F and preheat, lid closed for 15 minutes.
- Remove the plastic wrap from the beef brisket and arrange on the grill grate. Smoke meat for 3 to 4 hours.
- Remove from grill and wrap in foil making sure to seal very well. Place back on grill and continue cooking for another 3 to 4 hours or until a thermometer inserted in the thickest part of the meat registers an internal temperature of 204°F.
- Remove from grill and rest in foil for at least 30 minutes before slicing. If you want cold pastrami, allow to cool completely, refrigerate until chilled and then slice. Enjoy!

3.43 Ultimate Loaded Nachos
Ingredients:

- 1 Bag Tortilla Chips
- 1/2 Cup Fresh Salsa
- 1 Lb. Kielbasa Sausage, Cooked and Sliced
- 1 Cup Cooked Chicken Breast, Shredded
- 1 Lb. Tri-Tip, Cooked and Cubed
- 1/4 Cup Black Olives, Sliced
- 1 Small Jar Jalapeños, Sliced
- 1/4 Cup Scallions, Sliced
- 1-1/2 Cup Cheddar Cheese
- 1/2 Cup Sour Cream
- 1/2 Cup Guacamole
- 1/4 Cup Cilantro

Introductions:

- When ready to cook, set the Traeger to 375°F and preheat, lid closed for 15 minutes.
- On a large tray, spread the tortilla chips evenly. First sprinkle the salsa on chips, then the Kielbasa sausage, chicken, and tri-tip.
- Top nachos with scallions, jalapeños, olives, and lastly the cheese.
- Place tray on the grill and bake for approximately 10 to 15 minutes, or until cheese melts and the nachos are heated through.
- Serve with sour cream, guacamole and cilantro. Enjoy!

3.44 Grilled London Broil with Blue Cheese Butter
Ingredients:

- London Broil
- 1/4 Cup Soy Sauce
- 1/4 Cup Water
- 1 Small Onion, Coarsely Chopped
- 1 Clove Garlic, Minced
- 2 Tbsp Red Wine Vinegar
- 2 Tbsp Vegetable Oil or Extra Virgin Olive Oil
- 1 Tbsp Ketchup
- 1 Tsp Worcestershire Sauce
- 1 Tsp Black Pepper, Freshly Ground
- 1 Tsp Sugar
- 1 (2 Lbs.) Top Round London Broil Steak
- Traeger Beef Rub
- Blue Cheese Butter
- 8 Tbsp Butter, Softened
- 1 Scallion, Finely Minced
- 1/4 Cup Crumbled Blue Cheese
- 1 Tsp Worcestershire Sauce
- Black Pepper, Freshly Ground

Instructions:

- For the Marinade: In a small mixing bowl, whisk together the soy sauce, water, onion, garlic, red wine vinegar, oil, ketchup, Worcestershire sauce, pepper and sugar.
- Place the meat in a large resealable plastic bag and pour the marinade over it. Refrigerate for 6 hours to overnight.
- Remove steak from the refrigerator and let it come to room temperature.
- For the Blue Cheese Butter: In a small mixing bowl, combine the butter, scallion, blue cheese, Worcestershire sauce, and pepper. Mix to combine with a wooden spoon. Cover and refrigerate if not using immediately.
- When steak is at room temperature, discarding the marinade and pat dry with paper towels.
- Season on all sides with Traeger Beef Rub.
- When ready to cook, set temperature to 180°F and preheat, lid closed for 15 minutes.
- Lay the steak directly on the grill grate and smoke for 60 minutes.
- Transfer steak to a platter. Increase grill temperature to High and preheat with the lid closed.
- When grill is hot, return steak to the grill and cook until desired internal temperature, 130°F for medium-rare, about 15 to 20 minutes.
- Let meat rest for 3 minutes, before thinly slicing on a diagonal. Serve with the Blue Cheese Butter. Enjoy!

3.45 Smoked Chili Con Queso
Ingredients:

- 1 (2 Lb.) Block Velveeta Cheese
- 1 Lb. Smoked Gouda Cheese
- 1 (10 Oz) Can Original Rote
- 1 (10 Oz) Can Diced Rote Fire Roasted Tomatoes and Green Chiles
- 1 (10 Oz) Can Cream of Mushroom Soup
- 1 Lb. Hot Pork Sausage
- 4 Tbsp Traeger Coffee Rub
- 1/2 Cup Chopped Cilantro

Instructions:

- Heat a medium cast-iron skillet over medium-heat and fully cook pork sausage breaking into small chunks as you go. Drain and discard fat reserving the sausage.
- When ready to cook, start the Traeger according to grill instructions. Set the temperature to 350 degrees F and preheat, lid closed, for 10 to 15 minutes.
- Use a 4 to 5-quart cast iron Dutch oven or another oven safe dish. Divide the block of Velveeta into 5-6 large pieces and cut the smoked gouda into small 1-inch cubes.

- Add the canned **Ingredients:** including the liquid. Add the meat and the Traeger Coffee Rub last.
- Smoke the queso for 45 minutes on the Traeger stirring three to four times. Add most of the cilantro the last 5 minutes of smoking.
- Sprinkle remaining cilantro on the top before serving. Enjoy!

3.46 Smoked Italian Meatballs
Ingredients:

- 1 Tsp Pepper
- 1 Tsp Parsley
- 1 Tbsp Oregano
- 1 Tsp Crushed Red Pepper
- 1 Tsp Kosher Salt
- 1 Tsp Onion Powder
- 1/2 Cup Parmesan Cheese, Grated
- 1 Lb. Ground Italian Sausage
- 1 Lb. Ground Beef
- 2 Eggs
- 1 Tbsp Worcestershire Sauce
- 1/2 Cup Bread Crumbs

Instructions:

- In a large bowl, mix together all the **Ingredients:** with hands until combined.
- Once all **Ingredients:** are mixed, shape the mixture into 1 1/2" meatballs. Place on a parchment lined baking sheet leaving space between each meatball.
- When ready to cook, set temperature to 180°F and preheat, lid closed for 15 minutes. For optimal flavor, use Super Smoke if available.
- Place the meatballs directly on the grill grate and smoke for 20 minutes.
- Increase the grill temperature to 350°F and cook for an additional 10 minutes, or until the internal temperature reaches 165°F.
- Serve meatballs over spaghetti noodles and top with your favorite marinara sauce. Enjoy!

3.47 Smoked Brisket Pot Pie
Ingredients:

- 2 Cups Leftover Brisket, Chopped
- 2 Tbsp Butter
- 2 Carrots, Peeled and Chopped
- 1 Yellow Onion, Chopped
- 1 Clove Garlic, Minced
- 1/2 Cup Frozen Peas
- 1 Cup Pearl Onions, Blanched and Peeled
- 2 Cups Beef Stock
- 1 Sheet of Frozen Pastry Dough
- 1 Egg

Instructions:

- In a medium stock pot melt the butter. When the butter is hot, add the carrots and saute 10-15 minutes until lightly browned.
- Add onion and cook 5-7 minutes until tender and translucent. Add the garlic and saute 30 seconds more until fragrant.
- Stir in the peas, onions and chopped brisket. Add beef stock and bring to a simmer.
- Cook until the liquid is reduced and thick enough to coat the back of a spoon. If the sauce doesn't thicken, add a slurry of cornstarch until thickened. Season with salt and pepper to taste.
- Pour brisket mixture into an oven proof baking dish. Place the pastry dough over the top making cuts in the top to vent.
- Mix the egg in a small bowl and brush the top of the pastry with the egg wash.
- When ready to cook, set the temperature to 350°F and preheat, lid closed for 15 minutes
- Place directly on the grill grate and bake for 45 minutes until the top is lightly browned and bubbling.
- Let stand 10 minutes before serving. Enjoy!

Chapter 4: Lamp Recipes

4.1 Whole Rack of Lamb
Ingredients:

- 2 Lb. Rack of Grass-fed Lamb
- 1 Tbsp Kosher Salt
- 8 Cloves Fresh Garlic
- 1 Small Bunch Fresh Thyme
- 2 Tsp Olive Oil
- 1 Tsp Sherry Vinegar

Instructions:

- Process the fresh garlic and all the thyme leaves in your food processor with the salt, oil and vinegar. Rub this pasted all over the rack of lamb.
- When ready to cook, set the temperature to 450°F and preheat, lid closed for 15 minutes
- Lay the rack of lamb fat-side down on the grill and cook for 20 minutes. Turn over so the fat side is up and cook for an additional 10 minutes. Thermometer should be placed into the center of the lamb and should register 150-160°F.
- Let rest for 10 minutes. Slice the rack into chops and serve. Enjoy!

4.2 Slow Roasted Shawarma
Ingredients:

- 5.5 Lbs. Top Sirloin
- 5.5 Lbs. Boneless Skinless Chicken Thighs
- 4.5 Lbs. Lamb Fat
- 4 Tbsp Traeger Rub
- 2 Large Yellow Onions
- Pita Bread
- Topping Options: Cucumber, Tomatoes, Tahini, Pickles, Fries, Israeli Salad
- A Double Skewer
- A Cast Iron Griddle

Instructions:

- *Plan ahead! Assemble the shawarma stack the night before you plan to cook it.
- Slice all the meat and fat into ½" slices and place into 3 bowls (pro tip: it's easier to slice if they are all partially frozen).
- Season each bowl with Traeger Rub and massage the rub into the meat.
- Place half an onion on the bottom of each half skewer to make a firm base. then add 2 layers from each bowl at a time. Try to make the stack symmetrical, more or less. Then put the other 2 half onions at the top. Wrap in plastic wrap and refrigerate overnight.
- When ready to cook, set temperature to 275°F and preheat, lid closed for 15 minutes.
- Lay the shawarma directly on the grill grate and cook for about 3-4 hours, rotating at least once.

- Remove from grill and increase the temperature to 445°F. While the grill preheats, place a cast iron griddle directly on the grill grate and brush with olive oil.
- When the griddle is hot place the whole shawarma on the cast iron and sear 5-10 minutes per side. Remove from grill, slice off the edges, then repeat with remaining shawarma.
- Serve in pita bread with your favorite toppings like cucumber, tomatoes, tahini, pickles, fries or Israeli salad.
- Enjoy!

4.3 Roasted Leg of Lamb
Ingredients:

1 (7-8 Lb.) Leg of Lamb, Bone-In

1 Tbsp Garlic, Crushed

4 Cloves Garlic, Sliced Lengthwise

4 Sprigs Rosemary, Cut Into 1" Pieces

2 Tsp Olive Oil

2 Lemons

Salt and Pepper, To Taste

Instructions:

- Combine olive oil and the crushed garlic. Rub mixture on the leg of lamb.
- With a paring knife, make small 3/4-inch deep perforations in the lamb, about 2 dozen. Stuff the slivered garlic and cut rosemary sprigs into the perforations.
- Zest and juice the lemons, spreading the zest and juice evenly over the lamb. Season lamb with salt and pepper.
- When ready to cook, set temperature to High and preheat, lid closed for 15 minutes.
- Place the leg of lamb on the grill and cook for 30 minutes.
- Reduce grill temperature to 350°F and cook until the internal temperature reaches 130°F for medium-rare, about 60-90 minutes.
- Let the lamb rest for 15 minutes before carving. Enjoy!

4.4 Grilled Lamb Chops with Rosemary Sauce
Ingredients:

- 1/2 Cup Extra Virgin Olive Oil, Divided
- 1/4 Cup Onion or Shallot, Coarsely Chopped
- 2 Cloves Garlic, Coarsely Chopped
- 2 Tbsp Soy Sauce
- 2 Tbsp Balsamic or Sherry Vinegar
- 1 Tbsp Fresh Rosemary Needles
- 2 Tsp Dijon Mustard
- 1 Tsp Worcestershire Sauce
- Freshly Ground Black Pepper, As Needed

Instructions:

- In a small saucepan, sauté the onion and garlic in 1 tablespoon of olive oil over medium heat until softened and translucent. Do not let brown.
- Transfer to a blender jar. Add the soy sauce, vinegar, rosemary, mustard, and Worcestershire and blend. Season to taste with black pepper.
- Slowly drizzle in the remaining olive oil while the machine is running until the sauce is emulsified. Add a tablespoon of water if the sauce is too thick. Set aside.
- When ready to cook, set temperature to High and preheat, lid closed for 15 minutes.
- Brush the lamb chops on both sides with olive oil and season generously with salt and pepper.
- Grill until lamb chops reach an internal temperature of 135°F for medium-rare, about 4 to 6 minutes per side.
- Serve with the rosemary sauce for dipping. Enjoy!

4.5 Roasted Leg of Lamb with Red Wine Reduction
Ingredients:

- 1 (6-8 Lb.) Bone-In Leg of Lamb
- 10 Garlic Cloves, Peeled and Thinly Sliced
- 3 Tbsp Rosemary Leaves, Chopped
- 2 Tsp Thyme Leaves, Chopped
- 2 Tbsp Olive Oil
- 1 Tbsp Kosher Salt
- 1/2 Tsp Freshly Ground Pepper
- 1 Cup Red Wine
- 1 Tsp Kosher Salt
- 3 Tbsp Unsalted Butter

Instructions:

- Rinse lamb leg with water and pat dry. Using a sharp paring knife, create 20 1-inch slits all around the leg of lamb that are 1-inch deep. Place a sliver of garlic into each slit.
- Combine the chopped rosemary and thyme with the olive oil, salt, and pepper. Using your hands, coat the lamb evenly with the herb oil.
- Gently wrap lamb in saran wrap, place on a tray, and refrigerate for at least 4 hours to overnight. One hour before grilling, remove the lamb from the refrigerator.
- Remove the plastic wrap and place the lamb on a roasting rack above a large roasting pan. Pour the red wine and stock into the bottom of the pan, ensuring the liquid does not touch the meat. If it is close, only use half of the wine and stock.
- When ready to cook, set the temperature to High and preheat, lid closed for 15 minutes.
- Place the lamb in its roasting pan directly on the grill grate and roast for 20 minutes. Reduce the heat to 350°F and roast another hour or more, about 10 to 12 minutes per pound or until the temperature reaches 130°F when a meat thermometer is inserted into the thickest part of the leg away from the bone.
- Remove the meat from the grill and loosely tent with foil on a cutting board. Allow to rest for 15-20 minutes.
- Meanwhile strain the juices from the pan into a medium saucepan removing any excess fat that has dropped into the pan.
- Bring the juices to a boil, reduce to a simmer, and cook until it can coat the back of a spoon, about 10 minutes.
- Whisk in the butter and taste, adding more salt and pepper as needed.
- Carve the lamb and serve with the red wine jus. Enjoy!

4.6 Grilled Lamb Burgers with Pickled Onions
Ingredients:

- Pickled Onions
- 1/2 Red Onion, Thinly Sliced
- 6 Tbsp Lime Juice
- 1/2 Tsp Kosher Salt
- 1/2 Tsp Raw Cane Sugar
- Yogurt Sauce
- 1 Cup Greek Yogurt
- 2 Tbsp Lemon Juice
- 1 Garlic Clove, Minced
- 2 Tbsp Finely Chopped Herbs, Such as Mint, Dill and Parsley
- 1/2 Tsp Kosher Salt
- Lamb Burgers
- 1 Tbsp Olive Oil
- 1/2 Red Onion, Finely Diced
- 1 Lb. Ground Lamb
- 8 Oz Ground Pork
- 3 Tbsp Finely Chopped Mint
- 2 Tbsp Finely Chopped Dill
- 3 Tbsp Finely Chopped Parsley
- 4 Garlic Cloves, Minced

- 1 1/2 Tsp Ground Cumin
- 1 Tsp Ground Coriander
- 1 Tsp Kosher Salt
- 1/2 Tsp Freshly Ground Black Pepper
- 1 Sliced Tomato
- 6 Buns
- Sliced Cucumber
- Butter Lettuce

Instructions:

- To Pickle the Onions: Place the onion, lime juice, salt and sugar in a small bowl. Stir to combine, cover and let sit at room temperature for about 2 hours to soften. Refrigerate until ready to use.
- To make the Yogurt Sauce: In a small bowl, stir together the yogurt, lemon juice, garlic, herbs, and 1/2 tsp salt. Adjust the salt to taste. Cover and refrigerate until ready to serve, or for up to 2 days.
- To make the lamb burgers: In a small skillet over medium heat, warm the olive oil. Add the onion and cook, stirring frequently until softened, about 7 minutes. Transfer to a small plate to cool.
- In a large bowl, combine the lamb, pork, mint, dill, parsley, garlic, cumin, coriander, salt, pepper, and cooled onions. Gently mix with your hands. Do not overwork the meat.
- Divide the mixture into 6 equal balls. Press into patties and transfer to a parchment-lined baking sheet. If not cooking immediately, cover and refrigerate for up to 8 hours.
- When ready to cook, set the temperature to High and preheat, lid closed for 15 minutes.
- Place the burgers on the grill and cook until well-browned, about 2 to 3 minutes per side for medium-rare, or about 5 minutes per side for well done.
- Transfer burgers to a plate to rest for 5 minutes before serving.
- Place burgers on buns and top with a generous dollop of herbed yogurt sauce and some pickled onions.
- Add lettuce, sliced tomatoes or cucumbers if desired. Serve immediately. Enjoy!

4.7 Braised Lamb Shank
Ingredients:

- 4 Shanks Lamb
- Olive Oil, As Needed
- Traeger Prime Rib Rub
- 1 Cup Beef Broth
- 1 Cup Red Wine
- 4 Sprigs Fresh Rosemary and Thyme

Instructions:

- Season the lamb shanks liberally with Traeger Prime Rib Rub.
- When ready to cook, set the temperature to High and preheat, lid closed for 15 minutes.
- Place the shanks directly on the grill grate and cook for 20 minutes or until the exterior has browned.
- Transfer the shanks to a Dutch oven and pour in beef broth, wine, and add herbs. Cover with a tight-fitting lid and place back on the grill grate reducing the temperature to 325°F.
- Braise the shanks for 3-4 hours until the internal temperature is 180°F. Take care not to touch bone with the tip of the temperature probe or you will get a false reading.
- Carefully lift the lid and transfer the lamb and any accumulated juices to a platter or plates. Enjoy!

4.8 Greek Style Roast Leg of Lamb Recipe
Ingredients:

- One 6-7 Lbs. Leg of Lamb, Bone-In
- 8 Cloves Garlic
- 2 Sprigs Fresh Rosemary, Needles Stripped, Stems Discarded
- 1 Sprig (Or 1 Tsp. Dried) Fresh Oregano
- 2 Lemons, Juiced
- 6 Tbsp. Evo (Extra-Virgin Olive Oil)
- As Needed Coarse Salt (Kosher) And Black Pepper, Freshly Ground

Instructions:

- Using a paring knife, make a series of small slits in the leg.
- On a cutting board, finely mince the garlic, rosemary, and oregano with a chef's knife to make an herb and garlic paste. (Alternatively, put the garlic and herbs in a small food processor.)
- Stuff a small amount of the paste into each of the slits, driving it into the slit with a spoon handle or other utensil. Put the lamb on a rack inside a roasting pan. If desired, like the pan with foil for easier clean-up.
- Rub the outside of the lamb with the lemon juice, then the olive oil. Cover with plastic wrap and refrigerate for at least 8 hours, or overnight.
- Remove from the refrigerator and let the lamb come to room temperature.
- Remove the plastic wrap and season the lamb with salt and pepper. When ready to cook, start the Traeger grill on Smoke with the lid open until the fire is established (4 to 5 minutes). Set the temperature to 400F and preheat, lid closed, for 10 to 15 minutes.
- Roast the lamb for 30 minutes. Reduce the heat to 350F (300 if you have a manual controller) and continue to cook until the internal temperature in the thickest part of the meat - be sure the temperature probe is not touching bone - is about 140F for medium-rare, about 1 hour more, longer if you're cooking at 300F or prefer your lamb more well-done.
- Transfer the lamb to a cutting board and let rest for 15 minutes before slicing on a diagonal into thin slices.

4.9 Smoked Lamb Sausage
Ingredients:

- Smoked Lamb Sausage
- 2 Lb. Lamb Shoulder
- 1 Qty. (60 Inch) Hog Casing
- 1 Tbsp. Garlic
- 1 Tsp. Cumin
- 1 Tsp. Paprika
- 1/2 Tsp. Cayenne
- 2 Tbsp. Ground Fennel
- 1 Tbsp. Cilantro, Finely Chopped
- 1 Tbsp. Parsley, Finely Chopped
- 1 Tsp. Black Pepper
- 2 Tbsp. Salt
- Sauce
- 3 Cups Greek Yogurt
- 1 Lemon, Juiced
- 1 Clove Garlic
- 1 Cucumber, Peeled, Shredded, And Drained
- 1 Tbsp. Dill
- To Taste Salt & Pepper

Instructions:

- Cut the lamb shoulder into 2-inch pieces, and using a meat grinder, grind the meat.
- Lightly combine the lamb with all the spices in a bowl and refrigerate. It is important to refrigerate the ground lamb so the fat does not melt in order to give the sausage a good texture.
- Next, using a sausage horn, attach the hog casing and start to feed the sausage back through the grinder to fill the casing and twist into links. With a paring knife, prick holes all along the casing (this will allow steam to escape while cooking). Refrigerate. Combine all
- When ready to cook, start your Traeger on Smoke, with the lid open until the fire is established (4 to 5 minutes). Set the temperature to 225°F, place the prepared sausage on the grill grate and smoke it for 1 hour.
- Once the hour is up, remove the links from the grill and turn the grill up to High (450°F) and preheat (10-15 minutes). Once the grill has reached 450°F, place the links back on the grill and cook for 5 minutes on each side.
- Serve hot with yogurt sauce and roasted potatoes on the side. Enjoy!

4.10 Lamb Lollipops with Mango Chutney
Ingredients:

- Lamb Lollipops
- 6 Lamb Chops, Around 3/4-Inch-Thick, Frenched
- 2 Tbsp Olive Oil
- 1/2 Tsp Course Kosher Salt
- 1/2 Tsp Black Pepper, Freshly Cracked
- 2 Tbsp Fresh Mint, Chopped
- Mango Chutney
- 1 Mango, Peeled, Seeded and Chopped
- 3 Cloves Garlic, Chopped
- 1/2 Habanero Pepper, Seeded and Chopped, Or More to Taste
- 3 Sprigs Fresh Cilantro, Chopped
- 1 Tbsp Fresh Lime Juice
- 1 Teaspoon Salt
- 1/2 Tsp Pepper, Freshly Cracked

Instructions:

- If you can't purchase frenched lamb chops, using a sharp knife, cut and scrape the flesh and fat off the bone to make it look like a lollipop.
- Add all chutney Ingredients into a food processor and pulse about 15 times or until desired consistency; set aside. Chop mint and set aside.
- When ready to cook, start the Traeger grill on Smoke with the lid open until the fire is established (4 to 5 minutes). Set the temperature to High and preheat, lid closed, for 10 to 15 minutes.
- While grill preheats, on a baking sheet drizzle lamb lollipop with olive. Coat both sides. Season both sides with salt and pepper and allow to sit at room temperature for 5 to 10 minutes.
- Place the lamb pops directly on grill grate. Close lid and grill for 5 minutes. Flip over and grill for another 3 minutes or until a thermometer inserted into the thickest part of the meat registers an internal temperature of 130 degrees F.
- Remove from grill and allow to rest 10 minutes before serving.
- Spoon chutney over each lamb lollipop and sprinkle with fresh chopped mint. Enjoy!

4.11 Pistachio Crusted Lamb with Vegetables
Ingredients:

- Pistachio Crusted Lamb
- 2 Racks of Lamb
- 1 Tsp Herbs De Provence
- Salt and Ground Black Pepper, To Taste
- 1 Tbsp Vegetable Oil
- 2/3 Cups Pistachio Nuts, Chopped
- 2 Tbsp Dry Bread Crumbs
- 1 Tbsp Butter, Melted
- 1 Tsp Olive Oil
- 3 Tbsp Dijon Mustard
- Roasted Tri Color Carrots and Fingerling Potatoes
- 1 Lb. Fingerling Potato Medley
- 1 Bunch Tri Color Carrots, Peeled & Chopped
- 1 Tbsp Olive Oil
- 1/2 Tsp Kosher Salt
- 1/2 Tsp Ground Black Pepper
- 1 Clove Garlic, Minced
- 2 Tsp Fresh Time, Minced

Instructions:

- When ready to cook, start the Traeger grill on Smoke with the lid open until the fire is established (4 to 5 minutes). Set the temperature to High and preheat, lid closed, for 10 to 15 minutes.
- Pat the lamb dries with paper towels and generously season each rack of lamb with herbs de Provence, salt and black pepper.
- Peel carrots, cut into 1-inch pieces and add to a large mixing bowl. Add the potatoes, olive oil, salt, pepper, garlic, and thyme. Stir to combine.
- Place a large cast iron skillet on grill and add 1 tablespoon of vegetable oil. Close the lid and allow to preheat for 20 minutes.
- Place lamb in skillet and cook, browning on all sides, 6 to 8 minutes. Transfer lamb to a baking pan leaving skillet on grill and set aside.
- Stir pistachios, bread crumbs, butter, olive oil and a pinch of salt and black pepper in a bowl.
- Spread mustard on the fat-side of each rack of lamb. Pat pistachio mixture on top of mustard.
- Place racks of lamb directly on grill grate next to skillet. Add the seasoned potatoes to the skillet. Close lid and cook for 15 minutes.
- After 15 minutes, open the grill and stir the potatoes and carrots. Cover the racks of lamb loosely with foil.
- Continue cooking for another 5 to 10 minutes or until a thermometer inserted diagonally into the thickest part of the meat registers an internal temperature of 125 degrees F.
- Remove the lamb from grill with foil still intact and allow to rest for 10 minutes. Check potatoes with a fork to see if they are tender. If not, allow the potatoes and carrots to cook for another 5 minutes or until tender.
- Cut each rack of lamb into 4 double chops and serve with roasted carrots and potatoes. Enjoy!

4.12 Smoked Lamb Leg with Salsa Verde
Ingredients:

- Leg of Lamb
- 1 Leg of Lamb, Aitchbone Removed, Fat Trimmed To 1/4 Inch Thick, And Tied
- 1 Head of Garlic, Peeled
- 2 Tbsp Kosher Salt
- 2 Tbsp Fresh Rosemary, Chopped
- 1 Tsp Fresh Ground Black Pepper
- 1/4 Dry Red Wine, Or Beef Broth
- Green Garlic Salsa Verde
- 6 Green Garlic Cloves, Unpeeled
- 1 Tbsp Capers
- 1 Lb. Fresh Tomatillos, Husked, Rinsed
- 1 Small Onion, Quartered
- 5 Serrano Chiles
- 1/4 Cup Fresh Cilantro, Chopped
- 1 Tsp Sugar
- Kosher Salt to Taste
- 2 Tbsp Olive Oil
- 1 Cup Low Salt Chicken Broth
- 3 Tbsp Squeezed Lime Juice

Instructions:

- When ready to cook, start the Traeger grill on smoke with lid open until fire is established (4 to 5 minutes). Set the temperature to High and preheat, lid closed, for 10 to 15 minutes.
- Thread garlic onto skewer. Grill garlic, tomatillos, onion quarters, and chiles until dark brown spots form on all sides, about 9 minutes for onion, 6 minutes for tomatillos and chilies, and 4 minutes for garlic.
- Remove everything from grill and place the chiles directly into a Ziplock bag. Allow chiles to steam in bag for 15 minutes. Place a cast iron pan on grill, close lid and allow to preheat for 10 minutes.
- Peel garlic and remove skin from chiles. Coarsely chop the onion, chiles, and garlic. Transfer tomatillos, cappers and all vegetables into blender. Add cilantro and 1/2 teaspoon sugar. Puree until smooth. Season to taste with kosher salt.
- Add oil to preheated cast iron pan. Carefully add the tomatillo mixture and stir until slightly thickened, stirring often (about 2 minutes). Add broth and 2 tablespoons lime juice.
- Close lid and allow mixture to reduce until it measures about 2 1/2 cups (about 15-20 minutes). Season the Verde to taste with salt and more sugar and lime juice. Cool slightly, then cover and chill. Remove from grill and turn temperature dial to Smoke setting.
- Pat lamb dry and score fat by making shallow cuts all over with tip of a sharp small knife. Using a paring knife, make little incisions all over lamb and stuff with garlic cloves. Rub olive oil over lamb and liberally season with salt, pepper and rosemary. Let stand at room temperature for 30 minutes.
- Place leg of lamb in center of grill. Smoke lamb on the Smoke setting for 30 minutes.
- Increase temperature 350 degrees F and cook until a thermometer inserted into the thickest part of the meat registers 130 degrees F (about 1-1/2 hours).
- Transfer to a cutting board and let stand 15 to 25 minutes; the internal temperature will rise to 140 degrees F for medium-rare.
- Slice and serve with salsa Verde. Enjoy!

4.13 Armenian Style Lamb Shanks with Barley Risotto
Ingredients:

- 2 Tbsp Pomegranate Molasses
- 1/4 Cup Tomato Paste
- 1 Tbsp Garlic Powder
- 1 Tbsp Ground Cinnamon
- 1 Tsp Ground Fenugreek
- 1 Tsp Ground Cumin
- 1 Tsp Ground Cayenne
- 1 Tsp Ground Turmeric
- 3 Tbsp + 2 Tsp Kosher Salt
- 4 Lamb Hind Shanks
- 2 Qt Lamb or Beef Stock
- 1 Cup Pearled Barley
- 2 Tbsp Olive Oil
- 1 Medium Yellow Onion, Small Dice
- 1/2 Cup Grated Parmigiano Reggiano
- 2 Tbsp Butter

Instructions:

- In a small bowl, combine pomegranate molasses, tomato paste, garlic powder, cinnamon, fenugreek, cumin, cayenne, turmeric and 1 tbsp of the salt.
- Mix until the mixture turns into a uniform paste. Spice paste can be made up to a week in advance. Refrigerate if making ahead.
- Prepare lamb shanks by removing silver skin and large tendons. Evenly rub 1/4 of the spice paste on each shank and place shanks in refrigerator for at least 6 hours and up to 24 hours.
- To cook the lamb shanks: Place shanks in large cast iron skillet (or any oven proof vessel) and cover halfway with lamb stock.
- When ready to cook, start the Traeger grill on Smoke with the lid open until the fire is established (4 to 5 minutes). Set the temperature to 300 degrees F and preheat, lid closed, for 10 minutes.
- Cook for 7 to 8 hours turning shanks over every hour. Add more lamb stock to skillet as needed. Shanks are ready when the meat is tender and beginning to fall away from the bone.
- When the lamb is in its last hour of cooking, start the barley risotto. Heat 1 quart of the lamb or beef stock to a boil. Remove from heat and set aside.
- In a medium pot, heat olive oil and add onions to pot. Sauté onion until softened. Add barley and toast for about two minutes, stirring. Add 1 cup of stock, and the 2 tsp of salt.
- Cook, stirring occasionally, on low heat until the barley has fully absorbed the liquid. Repeat this step, adding 1/2 a cup of stock at a time until the barley is completely cooked through.
- Add parmigiano Reggiano and butter and stir to incorporate. Taste and add salt as needed.
- Serve lamb with barley risotto. Enjoy!

4.14 BBQ Lamb Wraps
Ingredients:

- Lamb
- 1 Leg of Lamb (6-7 Lb.)
- Juice of One Lemon
- Olive Oil
- Kosher Salt, To Taste
- Black Pepper, To Taste
- 1 Traeger Big Game Rub
- 12 Pitas
- 3 Roma Tomatoes, Sliced
- 1 Red Onion, Cut in Half and Sliced into Half Moons
- 8 Oz Feta Cheese, Crumbled
- Tzatziki Sauce
- 2 Cups Greek Yogurt
- 2 English Cucumbers Seeded and Finely Chopped
- 2 Cloves Garlic, Finely Minced
- Zest Of 2 Lemons
- Juice Of 2 Lemons
- 4 Tbsp Fresh Dill
- 2 Tbsp Fresh Mint
- Kosher Salt to Taste
- Black Pepper to Taste

Instructions:

- Remove from the refrigerator and let the lamb come to room temperature.
- Rub the outside of the lamb with the lemon juice, then the olive oil. Season with Traeger Big Game rub.
- When ready to cook, start the Traeger grill on Smoke with the lid open until the fire is established (4 to 5 minutes). Set the temperature to 400 degrees F and preheat, lid closed, for 10 to 15 minutes.
- Roast the lamb for 30 minutes. Reduce the heat to 350 degrees F and continue to cook until the internal temperature in the thickest part of the meat but not touching bone - is 140 degrees F for medium-rare.
- While lamb is roasting, combine all **Ingredients:** for tzatziki sauce in a mixing bowl and mix to combine. Place in fridge to chill.
- The last little bit of cooking, take the pittas and wrap in aluminum foil and place on grill to warm.
- Transfer the lamb to a cutting board and let rest for 15 minutes before slicing on a diagonal into thin slices.
- Build the wraps by filling a warm pitta with lamb, tzatziki sauce, diced tomato, red onion and feta crumble on top.
- Serve with fries and a side of the tzatziki. Enjoy!

4.15 Slow Roasted BBQ Lamb Shoulder
Ingredients:

- 1/4 Tsp Caraway Seeds
- 1/4 Tsp Coriander Seeds
- 1/4 Tsp Cumin Seeds
- 1 Tsp Dry Mint Leaves
- 2 Oz Ancho Chiles, Stemmed and Seeded
- 1 Tbsp Smoked Sweet Paprika
- 1 Tbsp Lemon Juice
- 3 Leg Garlic Cloves, 1 Clove Mashed to A Paste
- 1/4 Cup Extra Virgin Olive Oil
- Kosher Salt
- 3 Lb. Lamb Shoulder Roast on The Bone

Instructions:

- In a spice grinder, finely grind the caraway, coriander and cumin seeds.
- In a microwave-safe bowl, cover the ancho chilies with water and microwave on high for 2 minutes.
- Let cool slightly, then transfer soft chilies and 2 tablespoons of water to a blender. Add the grinded spices, paprika, lemon juice, the 2 garlic cloves, 2 tablespoons of the olive oil and 1 tablespoon of salt. Puree the harissa sauce until smooth.
- Set lamb in a medium roast pan and rub 1/2 cup of the harissa sauce all over the meat; let stand at room temperature for at least 2 hours.
- When ready to cook, start the Traeger grill on Smoke with the lid open until the fire is established (4 to 5 minutes). Set the temperature to 325 degrees F and preheat, lid closed, for 10 to 15 minutes.
- Add 1/2 cup of water to roasting pan and cover the pan loosely with foil. Cook the lamb for 2-1/2 hours, adding water to the pan a few times.
- Remove foil and cook for about 2-1/2 hours longer, until the lamb is brown and tender; occasionally spoon pan juices on top.
- Let stand for 20 minutes after removing from grill.
- Meanwhile, in a small bowl, combine the yogurt with cilantro, mashed garlic clove and 2 tablespoons of olive oil. Using a fork, pull the lamb off the bone in large chunks.
- Using your fingers, pull the lamb into smaller shreds and serve with the yogurt sauce and lettuce leaves, naan and the remaining harissa sauce. Enjoy!

4.16 Braised Lamb Shoulder Tacos
Ingredients:

- 3 Lb. Lamb Shoulder Roast
- 1/4 Tbsp Cumin Seeds
- 1/4 Tbsp Coriander Seeds
- 1/4 Tbsp Pumpkin Seeds
- 1 Tbsp Freshly Chopped Oregano
- 2 Oz Guajillo Peppers, Seeded
- 1 Tbsp Smoked, Sweet Paprika
- 1 Tbsp 1 T Lime Juice
- 3 Cloves Garlic, Roasted
- 1/4 Cup Evo
- Kosher Salt

Instructions:

- In a spice grinder, finely grind the seeds.
- In a microwave-safe bowl, cover the guajillo chilies with water and microwave on high for 2 minutes. Let cool slightly, then transfer soft chilies and 2 tablespoons of water to a blender.
- Add the ground spices, paprika, lime juice, oregano, the garlic cloves, 2 tablespoons of the olive oil and 1 tablespoon of salt. Puree the sauce until smooth.
- Set lamb in a medium roast pan and rub 1/2 cup of the sauce all over the meat; let stand at room temperature for at least 2 hours and up to 12 hours.
- When ready to cook, start the Traeger grill on Smoke with the lid open until the fire is established (4 to 5 minutes). Set the temperature to 325 degrees F and preheat, lid closed, for 10 to 15 minutes.
- Add 1/2 cup of water to roasting pan and cover the pan loosely with foil. Cook the lamb for 2-1/2 hours, adding water to the pan a few times.
- Remove foil and cook for about 2-1/2 hours longer, until the lamb is brown and tender; occasionally spooning the juices on top.
- Let stand for 20 minutes after removing from grill. Shred the meat when it's cool enough to handle and combine with remaining liquid in the bottom of the pan.
- Serve on corn tortillas, sprinkled with a squeeze of lime, sea salt, pickled radishes, and a sprig of cilantro. Enjoy!

4.17 Ultimate Grilled Lamb Burger
Ingredients:

- Roasted Red Pepper Mayo
- 1 Red Bell Pepper
- 1 Cup Mayo
- 2 Cloves Garlic
- 2 Tsp Fresh Lemon Juice
- 1 Tsp Kosher Salt
- 1/2 Tsp Black Pepper
- Ultimate Grilled Lamb Burger
- 2 Lb. Ground Lamb
- 1 Jalapeño, Seeded and Minced
- 6 Scallions, Minced
- 2 Tbsp Mint Leaves, Minced
- 2 Tbsp Dill, Minced
- 3 Cloves Garlic, Minced
- Kosher Salt and Black Pepper, To Taste
- 4 Slices Manchego Cheese
- 1 Cup Baby Arugula
- 1 Red Onion, Sliced
- 1 Large Ripe Tomato, Sliced
- 4 Brioche Buns

Instructions:

- When ready to cook, start the Traeger grill on Smoke with the lid open until the fire is established (4 to 5 minutes). Set the temperature to High and preheat, lid closed, for 10 to 15 minutes.
- Add the lamb, jalapeño, scallions, mint, dill, garlic, salt, and pepper to mixing bowl. Mix to combine.
- Form the lamb mixture into 4 to 8-ounce patties about ¾" inch thick. Set aside.
- Place the red bell pepper on preheated grill and cook for 20 minutes turning a quarter turn every 5 minutes or until it has charred a bit around the whole pepper.
- Remove the pepper from the grill and place in a large zip top bag and seal. After about 10 minutes, remove pepper from bag, cut in half, remove seeds and peel off skin.
- Add the roasted red pepper, mayo, lemon juice, garlic, salt and pepper to a food processor and process until smooth. Set aside.
- Place the lamb burgers on the grill still set to High, and cook for 5 minutes per side for medium or until desired doneness. The last minute of cooking, place your buns on the grill to toast and top burgers with a slice of cheese.
- Spread sides of toasted buns with mayo, add burgers to buns and top with arugula, onion and tomato. Serve with your favorite sides. Enjoy!

4.18 Grilled Lamb Kabobs
Ingredients:

- 3 Lbs. Boneless Leg of Lamb, Cut Into 2-Inch Cubes
- 1/2 Cup Olive Oil
- 1/2 Tbsp Kosher Salt
- 2 Tsp Freshly Ground Black Pepper
- 1/2 Cup Lemon Juice
- 1 Tbsp Lemon Zest
- 1 Tsp Cumin
- 2 Tbsp Fresh Mint, Chopped
- 1/2 Tbsp Fresh Cilantro, Chopped
- 2 Red Onions, Cut Into 8ths
- 15 Dried Apricots, Rehydrated
- 3 Traeger Flexible Skewers

Instructions:

- In a medium bowl, combine olive oil, salt, pepper, lemon juice, zest, cumin, mint and cilantro and mix well. Add lamb shoulder and toss to coat. Transfer to refrigerator and marinate over night.
- Remove lamb from marinade and thread lamb, apricots, and red onion alternating until the skewer is full.
- When ready to cook, start the Traeger grill on Smoke with the lid open until the fire is established (4 to 5 minutes). Set the temperature to 400 degrees F and preheat, lid closed 10-15 minutes.
- Lay skewers directly on the grill grate and cook for 8-10 minutes (for medium rare) or until the onions are lightly browned and lamb is cooked to desired temperature.
- Remove from grill and serve with your favorite side; quinoa, or rice are our favorites. Enjoy!

4.19 Roasted Rack of Lamb
Ingredients:

- 1 Rack (1-1/2 Lbs.) Lamb, Frenched
- 1/2 Cup Yellow Mustard
- 1 Tbsp Salt
- 1 Tsp Black Pepper, Ground
- 1 Cup Panko
- 1 Tbsp Italian Parsley, Minced
- 1 Tsp Sage, Minced
- 1 Tsp Rosemary, Minced

Instructions:

- Trim and clean the lamb if your butcher hasn't already done so. Rub the exterior with mustard and season generously with salt and pepper.
- In a shallow baking dish, combine breadcrumbs and herbs. Dredge the lamb in the breadcrumb mixture.
- When ready to cook, start the Traeger grill on Smoke with the lid open until the fire is established (4 to 5 minutes). Set the temperature to 450 degrees F (or 500 degrees F if using a WiFIRE enabled grill) and preheat lid closed for 10-15 minutes.
- Place the rack of lamb directly on the grill grate bone side down and cook for 20 minutes or until the internal temperature reaches 120 degrees F when an instant read thermometer is inserted into the thickest part of the lamb.
- Remove from the grill and let rest 5-10 minutes before slicing. Enjoy!

4.20 Grilled Butterflied Leg of Lamb
Ingredients:

- 1 Lemon, Juiced and Rinds Reserved
- 1/4 Cup Red Wine Vinegar
- 4 Cloves Garlic, Minced
- 2 Tbsp Fresh Or 2 Tsp Dried Rosemary, Minced
- 2 Tsp Fresh, or 1 Tsp Dried Fresh Thyme, Minced
- 1 Tsp Salt
- 1 Tsp Black Pepper, Freshly Ground
- 1 Cup Extra-Virgin Olive Oil
- 1 Onion, Sliced into Rings
- 1 (4-5 Lbs.) Leg of Lamb, Butterflied and Boneless

Instructions:

- For the Marinade: Cut the lemon into quarters and remove the seeds. Squeeze lemon juice into a mixing bowl and reserve the lemon rinds. Add the red wine vinegar, garlic, rosemary, thyme, salt and pepper and stir until the salt crystals dissolve. Whisk in the olive oil.
- Remove any netting from the lamb. Put the lamb into a large resealable plastic bag.
- Pour marinade into the bag, and add the onion and the reserved lemon rinds.
- Massage the bag to distribute the marinade and herbs. Refrigerate for several hours, or overnight.
- Remove the lamb from the marinade and pat dry with paper towels. Discard the marinade.
- When ready to cook, start the Traeger according to grill instructions. Set the temperature to High and preheat, lid closed, for 10 to 15 minutes.
- Arrange the lamb on the grill grate, fat-side down. Grill for 15 to 20 minutes per side or until the internal temperature reaches 135 degrees F for medium-rare.
- Let lamb leg rest for 5 minutes before slicing. To serve, slice thinly across the grain. Enjoy!

4.21 Braised Irish Lamb Stew
Ingredients:

- 4 Lbs. Lamb Shoulder, Boneless, Cut Into 1-Inch Pieces
- Salt and Pepper, To Taste
- 1/4 Cup Flour
- 1/4 Cup Butter, Room Temp
- 8 Oz Bacon, Chopped
- 2 Cloves Garlic, Minced
- 1/2 Cup White Wine
- 4 Cups Beef Stock
- 2 Bay Leaf
- 2 Sprigs Thyme
- 1 Sprig Rosemary
- 1 Onion, Small Dice
- 2 Carrots, Peeled, Cut Into 1/2-Inch Pieces
- 2 Large Potatoes, Peeled, 1/2-Inch Dice

Instructions:

- When ready to cook, start the Traeger on Smoke with the lid open until the fire is established (4 to 5 minutes). Set the temperature to 350 degrees F and preheat, lid closed, for 10-15 minutes.
- Season lamb with salt and pepper. Heat 2 Tbsp olive oil in a Dutch oven over medium heat. Brown lamb in batches and set aside.
- Add bacon and cook 15-20 minutes stirring occasionally until lightly browned. Remove bacon and discard all but 2 Tbsp of the bacon fat.
- Add fat back to the Dutch oven and onions and saute until translucent. Add garlic and cook 30 seconds more. Transfer lamb and bacon back to the pan and deglaze with white wine using a wooden spoon to scrape up all the browned bits on the bottom of the pan.
- Add stock, herbs, potatoes and carrots and bring to a simmer. Cover and transfer to the grill. Let stew cook for 1-1/2 to 2 hours or until the lamb is tender and falling apart.
- Remove stew from grill and place back on the stove top over medium heat. Mix butter and flour together in a small bowl and whisk into the stew. Let cook 5-10 minutes or until the stew is thick enough to coat the back of a spoon.
- Season with salt and pepper to taste. Remove bay leaves and springs from thyme and rosemary and serve. Enjoy!

Chapter 5: Chicken Recipes

5.1 Hellfire Chicken Wings
Ingredients:

- Hellfire Chicken Wings
- 3 Lbs. Chicken Wings
- 2 Tbsp. Vegetable Oil
- Rub
- 1 Tbsp. Paprika
- 2 Tsp. Brown Sugar
- 1 Tsp. Salt
- 1 Tsp. Black Pepper, Freshly Ground
- 1 Tsp. Cayenne Pepper
- 1 Tsp. Onion Powder
- 1 Tsp. Granulated Garlic
- 1 Tsp. Celery Seed
- Sauce
- 8 Tbsp. Butter, Unsalted
- 2 - 4 Jalapeno Peppers, Thinly Sliced Crosswise
- 1/2 Cup Cilantro Leaves
- 1/2 Cup Hot Sauce

Instructions:

- Cut the tips off wings and discard. Cut each wing into two pieces through the joint, giving you a meaty "drumette" and a "flat". Transfer to a large mixing bowl and pour the oil over the chicken
- Make the rub: In a small mixing bowl, combine the paprika, sugar, salt, black pepper, cayenne, onion powder, granulated garlic, and celery seed.
- Sprinkle over the chicken and toss gently with your hands to coat the wings.
- When ready to cook, set the temperature to 350°F and preheat, lid closed for 15 minutes
- Grill the wings for 35 to 40 minutes, or until the skin is crisp and golden brown and the chicken is cooked through, turning once halfway through the cooking time.
- Make the sauce: Melt the butter over medium-low heat in a small saucepan. Add the jalapeños and cook for 3-4 minutes. Stir in the cilantro & hot sauce.
- Pour the sauce over the wings and toss to coat. Enjoy!

5.2 Buffalo Chicken Thighs
Ingredients:

- 4-6 Boneless, Skinless Chicken Thighs
- 1 Cup Buffalo Wing Sauce
- 4 Tbsp. Butter
- Traeger Pork & Poultry Rub, As Needed
- Bleu Cheese Crumbles, For Serving
- Ranch Dressing, For Serving

Instructions:

- When ready to cook, set the temperature to 450°F and preheat, lid closed for 15 minutes.
- Generously season the chicken thighs with your desired Traeger seasoning and place directly on the grill grate. Cook for 8-10 minutes, flipping once.
- In a small saucepan, cook the wing sauce and the butter over medium heat stirring occasionally.
- Dip the cooked chicken thighs into the wing sauce and butter mixture, turning to coat both sides evenly.
- Return the sauced chicken thighs to the grill and cook for an additional 4-5 minutes or until the internal temperature reads 175 degrees on a meat thermometer.
- Sprinkle with the Bleu cheese and drizzle with the ranch dressing (optional). We like to serve ours as sliders on toasted buns with all the fixings. Enjoy!

5.3 Beer Braised Chicken Tacos with Jalapeño Relish
Ingredients:

- Jalapeño Relish
- 3 Jalapeños, Seeded and Diced
- 1/4 Cup Red Onion, Finely Diced
- 1 Clove Garlic, Minced
- 2/3 Cup White Wine Vinegar
- 1/3 Cup Water
- 1 Tbsp Sugar
- 1 Tbsp Salt
- Pickled Cabbage
- 2 Cups Shredded Red Cabbage
- 1/2 Cup White Wine Vinegar
- 1 Tbsp Salt
- 1 Tbsp Sugar
- Braised Chicken
- 2 Lbs. Boneless Skinless Chicken Thighs
- 1 Tbsp Olive Oil
- 1 Tsp Salt
- 1 Tsp Black Pepper
- 1/2 Yellow Onion, Small Dice
- 1 Jalapeño, Deseeded and Chopped
- 1 Clove Garlic, Minced
- 1 Tsp Chili Powder
- 1 Tsp Garlic Powder
- 4 Tbsp Adobo Sauce
- 1 Ea. Chipotle Chile In Adobo
- Juice Of 2 Limes
- 1 (12 Oz) Can Model Beer
- Tacos
- 8-12 Small Flour Tortillas
- Cotija Cheese
- Cilantro
- Your Favorite Hot Sauce

Instructions:

- For the jalapeño relish, combine all **Ingredients:** in a non-reactive dish and set aside.
- To make the pickled cabbage, combine all **Ingredients:** in a non-reactive dish and set aside.
- Transfer both the relish and pickled cabbage to the refrigerator and let sit a couple hours to overnight.
- Season chicken thighs generously with salt and pepper. Heat 1 Tbsp olive oil in a Dutch oven over medium-high heat. Place chicken thighs skin side down and brown in batches. Remove from heat and set aside.
- Add 1 Tbsp butter to the Dutch oven and set over medium-high heat. When butter is melted, add onion and jalapeño and sauté 3-5 minutes until translucent. Add minced garlic and sauté 30 seconds or until fragrant.
- Add chili powder, adobo sauce, chipotle chile and lime juice. Add chicken thighs back to the Dutch oven and pour in beer.
- When ready to cook, set the Traeger to 350°F and preheat, lid closed for 15 minutes.
- Place Dutch oven in the grill and braise for 30 minutes or until chicken is tender and falls apart. Remove chicken from braising liquid and shred.
- To build the tacos, place shredded chicken on tortilla, top with jalapeño relish, cabbage, cotija, cilantro, and finish with hot sauce. Enjoy!

5.4 Slow Roasted Shawarma
Ingredients:

- 5.5 Lbs. Top Sirloin
- 5.5 Lbs. Boneless Skinless Chicken Thighs
- 4.5 Lbs. Lamb Fat
- 4 Tbsp Traeger Rub
- 2 Large Yellow Onions
- Pita Bread
- Topping Options: Cucumber, Tomatoes, Tahini, Pickles, Fries, Israeli Salad
- A Double Skewer
- A Cast Iron Griddle

Instructions:

- *Plan ahead! Assemble the shawarma stack the night before you plan to cook it.
- Slice all the meat and fat into ½" slices and place into 3 bowls (pro tip: it's easier to slice if they are all partially frozen).
- Season each bowl with Traeger Rub and massage the rub into the meat.
- Place half an onion on the bottom of each half skewer to make a firm base. then add 2 layers from each bowl at a time. Try to make the stack symmetrical, more or less. Then put the other 2 half onions at the top. Wrap in plastic wrap and refrigerate overnight.
- When ready to cook, set temperature to 275°F and preheat, lid closed for 15 minutes.
- Lay the shawarma directly on the grill grate and cook for about 3-4 hours, rotating at least once.
- Remove from grill and increase the temperature to 445°F. While the grill preheats, place a cast iron griddle directly on the grill grate and brush with olive oil.
- When the griddle is hot place the whole shawarma on the cast iron and sear 5-10 minutes per side. Remove from grill, slice off the edges, then repeat with remaining shawarma.
- Serve in pita bread with your favorite toppings like cucumber, tomatoes, tahini, pickles, fries or Israeli salad.
- Enjoy!

5.5 BBQ Chicken Nachos
Ingredients:

- 1-1/4 Lbs. Chicken Breasts, Boneless, Skinless
- Traeger Pork & Poultry Rub, As Needed
- 1/2 To 3/4 Cup Traeger Qu BBQ Sauce
- 24 Large Tortilla Chips
- 3 Cups Mexican Blend Shredded Cheese
- 1/2 Cup Black Olives, Sliced and Drained
- Pickled Jalapenos, Sliced
- 3 Scallions, Thinly Sliced
- 1 Cup Sour Cream

Instructions:

- Season the chicken breasts with the Traeger Pork and Poultry Rub.
- When ready to cook, set temperature to 350°F and preheat, lid closed for 15 minutes.
- Arrange the chicken breasts on the grill grate and cook, turning once halfway through the cooking time, for 25 to 30 minutes, or until the internal temperature when read on an instant-read meat thermometer is 170°F. Transfer to a cutting board and let rest for 3 minutes. Leave the grill on if you are making the nachos immediately.
- Dice the chicken into small cubes, 1/2-inch or less. Transfer to a mixing bowl and pour 1/2 cup of Traeger Regular Barbecue Sauce over the diced chicken. Stir gently to coat each piece.
- Set aside, or cover and refrigerate if not making the nachos immediately. Lay the tortilla chips in a single layer on a rimmed baking sheet or pizza pan. Sprinkle evenly with half the cheese and a few of the jalapenos (if using).
- Spoon barbecued chicken mixture on each chip. Top with black olives and more pickled jalapeno, if desired. Sprinkle the remaining half of the cheese evenly over the chips. Scatter the sliced onions over the chips.
- Put the baking sheet on the grill grate. Bake until the chips are crisp and the cheese is melted, 12 to 15 minutes. With a spatula, transfer the nachos to a plate or platter. Serve immediately with sour cream and pickled jalapenos. Enjoy!

5.6 Spicy BBQ Chicken
Ingredients:

- 1 Whole Chicken
- 6 Thai Chiles
- 2 Tbsp Sweet Paprika
- 1 Scotch Bonnet
- 2 Tbsp Sugar
- 3 Tbsp Salt
- 1 White Onion
- 5 Garlic Cloves
- 4 Cups Grape Seed Oil

Instructions:

- Puree the Thai chilies, paprika, scotch bonnet, sugar, salt, onion, garlic, and grape seed oil together until smooth.
- Smother the chicken with mixture and let rest in fridge overnight.
- When ready to cook, set the Traeger to 300°F and preheat, lid closed for 15 minutes.
- Place chicken on grill breast side up and smoke for 3 hours or until it reaches an internal temperature of 165°F in the breast.
- Remove from grill and allow to rest for 10 to 15 minutes before slicing.Serve with sides of choice. Enjoy!

5.7 Traeger BBQ Half Chickens
Ingredients:

- 1 Ea. (3-3 1/2 Lb.) Young Fresh Chicken
- Traeger Apricot BBQ Sauce
- Traeger Summer Shandi Rub

Instructions:

- Place the chicken, breast side down, on a cutting board with the neck pointing away from you. Cut along one side of the backbone, staying as close to the bone as possible, from the neck to the tail.
- Repeat on the other side of the backbone then remove it. Open the chicken and slice through the white cartilage at the tip of the breastbone to pop it open. Cut down either side of the breast bone then use your fingers to pull it out.
- Flip the chicken over so it is skin side up and cut down the center splitting the chicken in half. Tuck the wings back of each chicken half.
- Season on both sides with Traeger Summer Shandi rub.
- When ready to cook, set the temperature to 375°F and preheat, lid closed for 15 minutes.
- Place chicken directly on the grill grate skin side up and cook until the internal temperature reaches 160 degrees F, about 60-90 minutes.
- Brush the BBQ sauce all over the chicken skin and cook for an additional 10 minutes.
- Remove from grill and let rest 5 minutes before serving. Enjoy!

5.8 Smoked Deviled Eggs
Ingredients:

- 7 Hard Boiled Eggs, Cooked and Peeled
- 3 Tbsp Mayonnaise
- 3 Tsp Chives, Diced
- 1 Tsp Brown Mustard
- 1 Tsp Apple Cider Vinegar
- Dash of Hot Sauce
- Salt and Pepper, To Taste
- 2 Tbsp Bacon, Crumbled
- Paprika, For Dusting

Instructions:

- When ready to cook, set temperature to 180°F and preheat, lid closed for 15 minutes. For optimal flavor, use Super Smoke if available.
- Place cooked and peeled eggs directly on the grill grate and smoke eggs for 30 minutes. Remove from grill and allow eggs to cool.
- Slice the eggs lengthwise and scoop the egg yolks into a gallon zip top bag. Add mayonnaise, chives, mustard, vinegar, hot sauce, salt, and pepper to the bag.
- Zip the bag closed and, using your hands, knead all of the **Ingredients:** together until completely smooth.
- Squeeze the yolk mixture into one corner of the bag and cut a small part of the corner off. Pipe the yolk mixture into the hardboiled egg whites.
- Top the deviled eggs with crumbled bacon and paprika. Chill until ready to serve. Enjoy!

5.9 Pickled Brined Hot Chicken Sandwich
Ingredients:

- Pickle Brined Chicken
- 2 Cups Leftover Pickle Juice
- 8 Ea. Boneless Skinless Chicken Thighs
- Salt and Pepper, As Needed
- 1 Cup Flour
- 1/2 Cup Tapioca Flour
- 1 Cup Buttermilk
- 2 Tsp Franks Red Hot Sauce
- 1 Egg
- Butter Hot Sauce
- 1/2 Cup Butter, Melted
- 1/2 Cup Franks Red Hot Sauce
- 2 Tsp Cayenne
- 1/2 Tsp Dark Brown Sugar
- 1 Tsp Black Pepper
- 1 Tsp Garlic
- 1 Tsp Paprika
- Sandwich
- Shredded Cabbage Slaw
- Traeger Smoked Pickles
- 4 Sesame Seed Buns

Instructions:

- In a medium bowl, combine pickle juice and chicken thighs. Weigh them down if necessary, to make sure they are completely submerged. Place in the refrigerator to brine overnight.
- When ready to cook, set the temperature to High and preheat, lid closed for 15 minutes.
- Place a cast iron pan with 1/2-inch canola oil on the grill grate while the grill preheats.
- Remove the chicken thighs from the pickle brine and pat dry.
- In a medium bowl combine both flours and a pinch of salt. Mix well to combine.
- In another bowl combine the buttermilk, hot sauce, egg and a pinch of salt. Mix well to combine.
- Season the chicken thighs with salt. Dip the thighs in the flour mixture, then buttermilk, then back into the flour mixture. Transfer to a wire rack and repeat with the remaining thighs.
- Place wire rack directly on the grill grate next to the cast iron of oil and bake chicken for 15 minutes or until the internal temperature reaches 150°F.
- As chicken pieces come to temperature, transfer them 2 or 3 at a time to the preheated oil to crisp the coating and finish cooking.
- For the Butter Hot Sauce: While the chicken is cooking, melt the butter and combine with the hot sauce, brown sugar, cayenne, garlic powder, paprika and black pepper in a medium bowl. Set aside.
- Remove chicken from the oil when the internal temperature reaches 165°F and dunk in the butter hot sauce mixture.
- Build the sandwiches with buns, mayonnaise, pickles, cabbage slaw and hot chicken. Enjoy!

5.10 Baked Chicken Cordon Bleu
Ingredients:

- 4 Ea. (4-5 Oz) Boneless, Skinless Chicken Breasts
- 8 Slices Prosciutto or Ham
- 8 Slices Swiss Cheese
- 1/3 Cup All-Purpose Flour
- Salt, As Needed
- Freshly Ground Black Pepper, As Needed
- 1 Cup Dry Breadcrumbs, Preferably Panko
- 1/4 Cup Grated Parmesan Cheese
- 2 Tbsp Melted Butter
- 2 Tsp Fresh Thyme Leaves
- 2 Eggs

Instructions:

- Spray a baking sheet with nonstick cooking spray. Set aside.
- Butterfly each chicken breast and place between two pieces of plastic wrap. Evenly pound with the flat side of a meat mallet, being careful not to tear the chicken, until chicken is 1/4-inch thick.
- Lay each chicken breast on a fresh piece of plastic wrap. Season chicken with salt and lay 1 to 2 slices of cheese on each breast followed by prosciutto or ham, then 1-2 more slices of cheese.
- Roll the chicken breast up like you would roll a burrito. Using the bottom piece of plastic wrap as an aid, fold the bottom of the breast up about an inch, then fold in the sides. Roll tightly.
- Wrap in the plastic wrap and tightly twist the ends to shape and compress the chicken. Repeat with the remaining chicken breasts. Chill in the refrigerator for 60 minutes.
- While chicken chills, season the flour with salt and pepper and put in a shallow dish.
- Combine the breadcrumbs, parmesan cheese, butter, and thyme. Season with salt and pepper and put in a second shallow dish.
- Whisk the eggs in a separate third dish.
- Arrange your workspace in this order: flour, eggs, breadcrumbs. Put the prepared baking sheet next to the breadcrumbs.
- Remove the plastic wrap from the chicken breasts. Coat each lightly with flour then dip in the egg.
- Finally, roll in breadcrumbs, patting them to make them adhere. Arrange on the baking sheet.
- When ready to cook, set the temperature to 375°F and preheat, lid closed for 15 minutes.
- Place the baking sheet with the chicken on the grill. Bake for 30-40 minutes, or until the coating is golden brown and the chicken is cooked through.
- Serve whole or slice crosswise into pinwheels with a sharp serrated knife. Enjoy!

5.11 Roasted Teriyaki Wings
Ingredients:

- 2 1/2 Lbs. Large Chicken Wings
- 1/2 Cup Soy Sauce
- 1/4 Cup Water
- 1/4 Cup Brown Sugar
- 2 Tbsp Rice Wine Vinegar
- 2 Scallions
- 1 Clove Garlic, Minced
- 2 Tsp Sesame Oil
- 2 Tbsp Fresh Ginger, Smashed
- 1 Tbsp Sesame Seeds, Lightly Toasted

Instructions:

- Cut the wings into three pieces through the joints. Discard the wing tips, or save for chicken stock.
- Transfer the remaining chicken drumettes and flats to a large resealable plastic bag or a bowl.
- For the Marinade: In a small saucepan, combine the soy sauce, water, brown sugar, vinegar, scallions, garlic, sesame oil, and ginger. Bring to a boil, then reduce the heat and simmer for 10 minutes.
- Cool completely, then pour over the chicken wings. Seal the bag and refrigerate for several hours, or overnight. Drain the wings, discarding the marinade.
- When ready to cook, set the temperature to 350°F and preheat, lid closed for 15 minutes.
- Cook for 45 to 50 minutes, or until the skin is brown and crisp and the meat is no longer pink at the bone.
- Turn once during the cooking time to prevent the wings from sticking to the grill grate. Remove from grill.
- Sprinkle with sesame seeds to serve. Enjoy!

5.12 Smoked Korean Wings
Ingredients:

- Brine
- 1 Gallon Water
- 1 Cup Sea Salt
- 1/2 Cup Sugar
- 1 Lemon, Halved
- 1 Head Garlic, Halved
- 4 Sprigs Thyme
- 10 Peppercorns
- Wings
- 3 Lb. Chicken Wings
- 2 Tbsp Olive Oil
- Sauce
- 1/2 Cup Gochujang Hot Pepper Paste#1
- 1/4 Cup Soy Sauce
- 1/3 Cup Honey
- 2 Tbsp Rice Wine Vinegar
- 2 Tbsp Fresh Squeezed Lime Juice
- 2 Tbsp Toasted Sesame Oil
- 1/4 Cup Butter, Melted
- 4 Cloves Garlic, Minced
- 1 Tbsp Ginger, Peeled and Grated

Instructions:

- For the Brine: To a stockpot, add 1 gallon of water, salt, and sugar, and stir well. Bring to a boil then remove from the heat and stir in the lemon, garlic, thyme, and peppercorns. Cool to room temperature, then submerge the wings. Cover and refrigerate for 2 to 4 hours.
- When ready to cook, set the temperature to 375°F and preheat, with the lid closed for 15 minutes.
- Remove the wings from the brine and dry them completely with paper towel. Discard brine.
- Toss the wings with the olive oil coating them completely.
- Place the wings directly onto the grill grate and cook to an internal temperature of 165°F, about 45 to 60 minutes.
- For the Sauce: In a bowl, combine all the sauce **Ingredients:** and whisk until smooth. Heat over medium-heat until the sauce just comes to a simmer, then remove from heat and set aside.
- Toss the cooked wings with 2/3 of the sauce, the green onions, peanuts, and sesame seeds.
- Serve wings with fresh cilantro, lime wedges, and extra sauce for dipping. Enjoy!

5.13 Roasted Buffalo Wings
Ingredients:

- Chicken Wings
- 4 Lbs. Chicken Wings
- 1 Tbsp Corn Starch
- Traeger Chicken Rub, As Needed
- Kosher Salt, To Taste
- Buffalo Sauce
- 1/4 Cup Spicy Mustard
- 1/2 Cup Franks Red Hot Sauce
- 6 Tbsp Unsalted Butter

Instructions:

- When ready to cook, set the temperature to 375°F and preheat, lid closed for 15 minutes.
- While grill is preheating, dry off chicken wings with a paper towel. Place wings in a large bowl and sprinkle with cornstarch, Traeger Chicken Rub and salt to taste. Mix to coat both sides of the chicken wings.
- When the grill has heated, place the wings on the grill and cook for 35 minutes total, turning halfway through cook time.
- Check the internal temperature of the wings at 35 minutes. The internal temperature should be at least 165°F. However, an internal temperature of 175-180°F will yield a better texture.
- For the Buffalo Sauce: In another pot add the Franks Red Hot, mustard and butter. Whisk to combine and heat through on the stove top.
- Keep sauce warm while the wings are cooking. When wings are done, pour the buffalo sauce over the wings, turning with tongs to coat.
- Cook for an additional 10-15 minutes on the grill for the sauce to set.
- Serve wings with ranch or blue cheese dressing. Enjoy!

5.15 Roasted Tequila-Lime Wings
Ingredients:

- Wings
- 3 Lbs. Chicken Wings
- 2 Tsp Ancho Chile Powder
- 2 Tsp Brown Sugar
- 1 Tsp Granulated Garlic
- 1 Tsp Cumin
- 1 Tsp Kosher Salt
- 1 Tsp Chili Powder
- 2 Tbsp Vegetable Oil
- Glaze
- 1/4 Cup Honey
- 1/4 Cup Pineapple Juice
- 3 Tbsp Tequila
- 1-1/2 Tbsp Hot Sauce
- 1-1/2 Tbsp Butter
- 1-1/2 Tbsp Fresh Lime Juice

Instructions:

- When ready to cook, set temperature to High and preheat, lid closed for 15 minutes.
- If you bought whole chicken wings, remove the tip and separate the drumettes and wings from each other. Pat them dry. Discard the wing tips or save them for chicken stock.
- Combine all of the dry rub **Ingredients** in a medium bowl. Add the oil and whisk to combine. Add the chicken wings and toss well to coat.
- For the Glaze: Combine glaze **Ingredients** in a small saucepan. Bring to a boil over medium heat. Cook until mixture is reduced by about 1/3 and begins to thicken, about 3 minutes. Keep the syrup warm while waiting to glaze.
- Place the wings directly on the grill grate and cook, turning once, until the internal temperature of the wings reaches 155-160°F, about 20 minutes.
- Brush the wings with the glaze and continue to cook until the internal temperature reaches 165-175°F, about 5-10 minutes longer.
- Serve warm. Enjoy!

5.16 Smoked Chicken Tikka Masala
Ingredients:

- Marinade
- 6 Garlic Cloves, Minced
- 1 Thumb-Sized Knob of Ginger, Finely Diced
- 4 Tsp Ground Turmeric
- 2 Tsp Garam Masala
- 2 Tsp Ground Coriander
- 2 Tsp Ground Cumin
- 2 Tsp Ground Chili
- 1 1/2 Cups Whole Milk Yoghurt
- 1 Tbsp Kosher Salt
- 2 Lb. Chicken Breasts, Cut Into 1-Inch Strips
- Tikka Masala Sauce
- 3 Tbsp Ghee or Clarified Butter
- 1 Medium Onion, Finely Diced
- Finely Diced Cilantro Stems 1/4 Cup
- Tomato Paste 1/4 Cup
- 6 Cardamom Pods, Crushed
- 1 (28 Oz) Can Crushed Tomatoes
- 2 Cups Heavy Whipping Cream
- 1-2 Sliced Fresh Chilies, For Garnish
- 1/2 Cup Fresh Cilantro, For Garnish
- 1 Cup Creamy Yogurt
- Cooked Basmati Rice, To Serve

Instructions:

- Prepare the spice mixture by combining the garlic, ginger and all the spices in a small bowl. Mix well and set aside.
- For the Marinade: In a large bowl, combine the sliced chicken breast, yogurt, 1/2 the spice mixture, and kosher salt. Mix well.
- Cover with plastic wrap and chill in the fridge overnight for marinated chicken perfection.
- When ready to cook, set the temperature to High and preheat with the lid closed for 15 minutes.
- For the Sauce: Heat a high-sided, oven-safe pan over medium-heat and melt the ghee. Add the onion, cilantro stems, cardamom, and a pinch of salt, and cook until the onion softens, about 5 minutes. Add the tomato paste and remaining spice mixture, and cook for 2 minutes. Pour in the tomatoes and season with another pinch of salt. Bring the sauce to a simmer and cook for about 8 minutes, until thickened.
- While the sauce is cooking, add the marinated chicken pieces to the grill and cook for 2 minutes per side, until just starting to turn to beautifully golden brown. Remove and set aside.
- Reduce grill heat to 350°F. Stir the cream into the sauce mixture, then fold in the chicken. Transfer the curry to the grill and cook, lid closed, for 35 to 40 minutes, until the chicken is cooked through and the curry is thick and glorious.
- Divide the cooked basmati rice onto plates, then top with curry. Garnish with yogurt, fresh chilies and cilantro. Enjoy!

5.17 Roasted Rosemary Orange Chicken
Ingredients:

- 1 (3-4 Lbs.) Chicken, Backbone Removed
- 1/4 Cup Olive Oil
- 2 Oranges, Divided
- Zest Of 1 Orange
- 2 Tsp Dijon Mustard
- 3 Tbsp Chopped Rosemary Leaves
- 2 Tsp Kosher Salt

Instructions:

- Rinse the chicken and pat dry with paper towels.
- For the Marinade: In a medium bowl, combine the olive oil, juice from the oranges (about 1/4 cup of freshly squeezed juice), the orange zest, Dijon mustard, rosemary leaves and salt. Whisk to combine.
- Place the chicken in a shallow baking dish large enough to be fully opened in one piece.
- Pour the marinade over the chicken ensuring it is covered with the marinade. Cover with plastic wrap and refrigerate for a minimum of 2 hours or up to overnight, turning once during the process.
- When ready to cook, set temperature to 350°F and preheat, lid closed for 15 minutes.
- Remove the chicken from the marinade and place on the grill, skin side down. Cook for 25-30 minutes until the skin is well-browned, then flip.
- Continue to grill chicken until the internal temperature of the breast reaches 165°F and the thigh reaches 175°F, about 5-15 minutes longer.
- Let rest 10 minutes before carving. Enjoy!

5.18 Loaded Grilled Chicken Tacos
Ingredients:

- Grilled Chicken
- 2 Lbs. Boneless-Skinless Chicken Breasts
- 2 Tbsp Olive Oil
- 2 Tsp Chili Powder
- 1 Tsp Smoked Paprika
- 1/2 Tsp Ground Cumin
- 1/4 Tsp Ground Cayenne
- 1 1/2 Tsp Kosher Salt Kosher Salt
- 1 Tsp Fresh Cracked Black Pepper
- Pico De Gallo
- 1 1/2 Lbs. Ripe Plum Tomatoes, Diced
- 1 Medium Red Onion, Diced
- 1/2 Cup Fresh Cilantro Leaves, Chopped
- Juice Of 1 Lime
- Kosher Salt, To Taste
- Guacamole
- 2 Ripe Avocados
- 1 Tbsp Fresh Squeezed Lime Juice
- 1/4 Cup Finely Diced Red Onion
- 2 Tbsp Finely Chopped Cilantro Leaves
- 1/2 Cup Sour Cream
- 1 Tsp Chili Powder
- 1 Tbsp Fresh Squeezed Lime Juice
- Pinch of Kosher Salt
- Toppings
- 10-12 Flour Tortillas
- 1 Lime, Cut into Wedges
- 1-2 Jalapenos, Sliced
- Handful of Fresh Cilantro
- Hot Sauce

Instructions:

- For the Marinade: Combine the chicken breasts, olive oil, spices, zest, salt, and pepper in freezer bag and give everything a good mix. Chill in the fridge for at least 4 hours (overnight is best).
- When ready to cook, set temperature to High and preheat, lid closed for 15 minutes.
- Place the chicken breasts on the hot grill and cook, lid closed, for 25 to 30 minutes, until crispy, golden, and the chicken reaches an internal temperature of 165°F.
- Rest the grilled chicken for 5 minutes before slicing into thin strips.
- While the chicken is on the grill, prepare the Pico, guacamole, and spiked sour cream.
- For the Pico: Combine all the Pico **Ingredients** in a small bowl and mix well. Set aside.
- For the Guacamole: Peel and carefully remove the pit from the avocados. Smash the avocado in a bowl until smooth, leaving a few chunks for texture, then add the remaining guacamole **Ingredients** and give everything a good mix.
- For the Spiked Sour Cream: Combine all the spiked sour cream **Ingredients** in a small bowl and mix well.
- Divide the sliced grilled chicken on warm tortillas, then hit each with fresh Pico, guacamole, and a dollop of spiked-sour cream.
- Top each taco with sliced jalapeño and fresh cilantro, and serve with lime wedges and hot sauce. Enjoy!

5.19 Grilled Thai Chicken Burgers with Papaya Slaw
Ingredients:

- Papaya Slaw
- 6 Oz Shredded Green Papaya (From 1 Medium Papaya)
- 1/2 Red Onion, Thinly Sliced
- 2 Tsp Grated Lime Zest
- 3 Tbsp Plus 2 Tsp Fresh Lime Juice
- 1 Tbsp Fish Sauce
- 1 Tbsp Brown Sugar
- Chicken Burger
- 1 Lb. Ground Chicken Thigh Meat
- 1/2 Cup Panko or Gluten Free Bread Crumbs
- 1/4 Cup Coconut Cream (Thick Milk Solids From 1 Can Chilled Coconut Milk)
- 1/2 Cup Chopped Fresh Cilantro
- 2 Garlic Cloves, Minced
- 2 Tsp Kosher Salt
- 1 Tsp Ground Cumin
- 1 Tsp Freshly Ground Black Pepper
- 1/2 Tsp Ground Ginger
- 1/2 Cup Mayonnaise
- 1 1/2 Tsp Curry Powder
- 1 Tbsp Vegetable Oil
- 8 Large Leaves Butter Lettuce Or 4 Hamburger Buns

Instructions:

- For the Papaya Slaw: In a medium bowl, combine the papaya, onion, 3 Tbsp of the lime juice, fish sauce and the brown sugar. Cover and refrigerate until ready to use, up to 3 hours.
- In a large bowl, stir together the ground chicken, breadcrumbs, coconut cream, cilantro, garlic, ginger, salt, pepper, cumin, lime zest, and remaining 2 tsp lime juice until thoroughly combined. Refrigerate for 20 minutes. If the mixture seems too wet or dry adjust with breadcrumbs or coconut milk until it stays together.
- Meanwhile, in a small bowl, stir together the mayonnaise and curry powder. Set aside.
- When ready to cook, set temperature to High and preheat, lid closed for 15 minutes.
- Using your hands, form the chicken mixture into four equal patties.
- Brush each burger with the vegetable oil on both sides. Cook for 4-5 minutes per side, or until the burgers reach 165°F internally. Remove from the grill and allow to rest for a few minutes before serving.
- Place each burger on a leaf of lettuce then top with curry mayonnaise and pickled papaya slaw. Top with a second lettuce leaf and serve.
- Alternatively, use regular hamburger buns and pile high with the burgers, curry mayonnaise and papaya slaw. Enjoy!

5.20 Baked Buffalo Chicken Dip
Ingredients:

- 1 (8 Oz) Package Cream Cheese, Softened
- 1/2 Cup Sour Cream
- 1/2 Cup Mayonnaise
- 2 Tbsp Dry Ranch Seasoning
- 1 Tsp Kosher Salt
- 1/2 Cup Franks Red Hot Sauce
- 2 Cups Chicken, Cooked and Shredded
- 1 Cup Cheddar Cheese, Shredded
- 1 Cup Mozzarella Cheese, Shredded
- Blue Cheese, To Taste
- Crumbled Bacon, To Taste

Instructions:

- When ready to cook start the Traeger grill on Smoke with the lid open until fire is established (4-5 minutes). Set the temperature to 350 degrees F and preheat, lid closed for 10-15 minutes.
- In the bowl of a stand mixer, combine cream cheese, sour cream, mayonnaise, ranch, salt, and hot sauce and mix with the paddle attachment until combined.
- Fold together the cheddar and mozzarella cheese and shredded chicken. Transfer to an oven proof dish and top with blue cheese and crumbled bacon.
- Place directly on the grill grate and cook for 20-30 minutes until the top is golden brown and dip is bubbling.
- Serve with chips, crackers, crostini, or sliced vegetables. Enjoy!

5.21 Tomatillo Braised Chicken
Ingredients:

- Tomatillo Salsa
- 1 Lb. Tomatillos, Husks Removed and Rinsed
- 1 White Onion, Quartered Through the Root End and Skin Removed
- 3 Jalapeños, Halved Lengthwise, Seeded If Preferred
- 2 Tbsp Olive Oil
- Kosher Salt
- 3 Tbsp Lime Juice
- 2 Tbsp Chopped Cilantro
- Braised Chicken
- 8 Bone-In, Skin-On Chicken Thighs
- 6 Bone-In, Skin-On Chicken Breasts
- Kosher Salt
- Freshly Ground Pepper
- 1/2 Cup Chicken Stock
- 2 Cups Tomatillo Salsa

Instructions:

- When ready to cook, set the temperature to 350°F and preheat, lid closed for 15 minutes.
- Place the tomatillos, onion, and jalapeños in a large bowl and add the olive oil and 1/2 tsp salt. Toss to coat evenly, then place in a grilling basket or a baking sheet.
- Grill, turning the vegetables occasionally, until they begin to char and soften, about 5 to 10 minutes. Remove the vegetables from the grill as they are ready.
- Transfer to the same bowl to catch their juices and allow them to cool to room temperature.
- Place the cooled vegetables along with their juices in a blender and add the lime juice, cilantro, and another pinch of salt. Pulse until the mixture reaches the texture of a salsa. Taste, adding more salt or lime juice as desired.
- Rinse the chicken and pat dry with paper towels. Sprinkle with salt and pepper on both sides.
- Place the chicken skin side down on the grill grate and cook until the skin is golden brown and very crispy, 10-15 minutes. Turn, cooking the other side for 5 minutes, then transfer the chicken to a plate.
- Place the grilled chicken legs in a Dutch oven or cast iron and add chicken stock and salsa Verde. Cover the pan and place directly on the grill grate.
- Cook for 1 1/2 to 2 hours until the chicken is fork tender. Enjoy!

5.22 Grilled Sticky Ginger Chicken Thighs
Ingredients:

- Marinade
- 1/2 Cup Grated Onion
- 1/2 Cup Peanut Oil
- 1/3 Cup Rice Vinegar
- 2 Tbsp Water
- 2 Tbsp Grated Fresh Ginger
- 2 Tbsp Ketchup
- 4 Tsp Soy Sauce
- 2 Tsp Sugar
- 2 Tsp Lemon Juice
- 1/2 Tsp Minced Garlic
- Chicken Thighs
- 4-6 Chicken Thighs
- 3 Green Onion Stalks
- 2 Limes
- Sesame Seeds, To Garnish

Instructions:

- Combine all sauce **Ingredients:** in a large bowl and set aside.
- Place chicken thighs into a zip lock bag and add approximately 3/4 of the dressing to cover. Place in the refrigerator to marinate for at least 1 hour.
- When ready to cook, set temperature to High and preheat, lid closed for 15 minutes.
- Place marinated chicken thighs on the grill grate, skin side down. Cook for 10 minutes, flip and cook another 10 minutes.
- Cut limes and green onions and place on chicken. Cook for an additional 5 minutes. Enjoy!

5.23 BBQ Game Day Chicken Wings and Thighs
Ingredients:

- 8-10 Chicken Thighs
- 20-30 Chicken Wings
- 1/2 Cup Olive Oil
- 1/2 Cup Traeger Chicken Rub

Instructions:

- When ready to cook, set the Traeger to 375°F and preheat, lid closed for 15 minutes.
- Place thighs and wings in a large bowl. Add the olive oil and Traeger Chicken rub and mix well. Cover bowl and refrigerate for 3 to 8 hours.
- Place chicken directly on the grill grate and cook for 45 minutes. Check the internal temperature of the chicken, it is considered done at 165°F however, a finished temperature of 175 to 180°F results in a better texture in dark meat.
- Once the finished temperature is reached, remove chicken from the grill and let rest for 5 to 10 minutes before serving. Enjoy!

5.24 Baked Garlic Parmesan Wings
Ingredients:

- Chicken Wings
- 5 Lbs. Chicken Wings
- 1/2 Cup Traeger Chicken Rub
- Sauce
- 1 Cup Butter
- 10 Cloves Garlic, Finely Diced
- 2 Tbsp Traeger Chicken Rub
- Garnish
- 1 Cup Parmesan Cheese, Shredded
- 3 Tbsp Parsley, Chopped

Instructions:

- When ready to cook, set temperature to High and preheat, lid closed for 15 minutes.
- In a large bowl, toss the wings with the Traeger Chicken rub.
- Place wings directly on the grill grate and cook for 10 minutes. Flip wings and cook for an additional 10 minutes. Check the internal temperature of the wings, finished desired temperature is 165-180 degrees F.
- To make the Garlic Sauce: While the chicken is cooking, combine butter, garlic and remaining rub in a medium sized saucepan and cook over medium heat on a stove top. Cook sauce for 8-10 minutes, stirring occasionally.
- When wings are finished cooking, remove from grill and place in a large bowl. Toss wings with the garlic sauce, parmesan cheese and parsley. Enjoy!

5.25 Roasted Habanero Wings
Ingredients:

- 4 Lbs. Chicken Wings
- 1 White Onion, Peeled and Chopped
- 2/3 Cup Sliced Green Onions, White and Light Green Parts Only, Plus 2 Tbsp for Garnish
- 2 Cloves Garlic, Peeled and Minced
- 1/4 Cup Vegetable Oil
- 2 Tbsp Low-Sodium Soy Sauce or Tamari
- 2 Tbsp Habanero or Other Hot Pepper Sauce
- 1-1/2 Tsp Salt
- 1-1/2 Tsp Ground Allspice
- 1 Tsp Ground Black Pepper
- 1/2 Tsp Dried Thyme
- 1/2 Tsp Ground Cinnamon
- 1 Habanero Pepper, Seeds Removed

Instructions:

- Cut off the tips of the wings and discard or save for making stock. Cut the wings into drumette and flat sections.
- To make the Marinade: Combine the onion, green onions and scallions in a food processor and puree until it is the texture of a thick paste. Add the oil, soy sauce, hot pepper sauce, the salt and all of the spices, and half or all of the habanero pepper, depending on how much heat you prefer. Process until all **Ingredients** are combined. Reserve some of the marinade for basting and set aside.
- Arrange the wings in a shallow baking dish and pour the marinade over the wings, tossing with tongs to ensure wings are evenly coated in sauce. Cover and refrigerate wings. Allow them to marinate for at least 6 hours or up to overnight, turning the wings at least twice.
- When ready to cook, set the Traeger to 350°F and preheat, lid closed for 15 minutes.
- Remove the wings from the marinade and discard what is left of the marinade.
- Place the wings directly on the grill grate and cook for 30 minutes, baste the wings with the reserved marinade and flip.Close the lid and continue cooking for another 20 minutes, or until the wings are browned and crispy and have reached an internal temperature of at least 165°F.Garnish wings with the remaining green onions and serve immediately.

5.26 Smoked Chicken Tikka Drumsticks
Ingredients:

- Chicken Tikka Drumsticks
- 1 Tbsp Smoked Paprika
- 1 Tbsp Garam Masala
- 1 Tbsp Ground Cumin
- 1 Tbsp Ground Coriander
- 1 Tsp Turmeric
- 1 Tsp Ground Cayenne
- 1/2 Medium Spanish Onion, Diced
- 1 Thumb-Sized Piece of Ginger, Peeled and Roughly Chopped
- 6 Cloves Garlic, Chopped
- 1/2 Cup Greek Yogurt
- Juice Of 1/2 A Lemon
- 1/4 Cup Olive Oil
- 12 Chicken Drumsticks
- Curry Lime Yogurt
- 1-1/2 Cups Greek Yogurt
- 1 Tbsp Curry Powder
- 1 Tbsp Fresh Squeezed Lime Juice
- Pinch of Sea Salt
- Garnishes
- Fresh Cilantro
- 1/2 Small Red Onion, Thinly Sliced
- 1 Lime, Cut into Wedges
- 1-2 Sliced Green or Red Chilies

Instructions:

- For the Marinade: In the base of a food processor, combine the spices, ginger, garlic, onion, yogurt, lemon juice, oil, and salt, and pulse until smooth.
- Place the chicken in a large bowl, pour over the marinade, then massage chicken until every nook and cranny of the chicken is coated. Cover with plastic wrap and chill in the fridge overnight (at least 12 hours).
- When ready to cook, set the temperature to High and preheat, lid closed for 15 minutes.
- Place the chicken directly on the grill grates and cook for 45-50 minutes, until crispy and wood-fire grilled to perfection (or until it reaches an internal temperature of 165°F).
- For the Curry Lime Yogurt: While the chicken is grilling, combine all of the yogurt **Ingredients** in a small bowl and mix well. Chill in the fridge until ready to serve.
- Garnish with fresh cilantro and sliced red onion and serve with curry lime yoghurt, fresh lime wedges, and if you like it extra spicy, sliced chilies. Enjoy!

5.27 Lemon Rosemary Beer Can Chicken
Ingredients:

- 1 (3-3.5 Lbs.) Whole Chicken
- 1 Lemon
- 1 Tsp Kosher Salt
- 1 Tsp Ground Pepper
- 1 Tsp Fresh Rosemary, Chopped Fine
- 1 (12 Oz) Can Beer

Instructions:

- When ready to cook, set temperature to High and preheat, lid closed for 15 minutes.
- Coat the chicken inside and out with the juice from one lemon. In a small bowl, combine the salt, pepper and rosemary and sprinkle on the inside and out of chicken.
- Empty half of the beer from the can and place the can on a solid surface. Place the chicken atop the beer can tucking the legs in the front.

- Carefully place the chicken directly on the grill grate using the legs to support if needed. Alternatively, place the chicken atop the beer can on a sheet tray for a more stable surface, then place the sheet tray directly on the grill grate.
- Cook the chicken until an instant read thermometer reads 165°F when inserted in the thickest part of the breast, about 60 minutes.
- Let the chicken rest 10 minutes before carving.
- Serve with Chardonnay or any of your favorite medium body red or white wines. Enjoy!

5.28 Ultimate Traeger Thanksgiving Sandwich
Ingredients:

- 1 French Bread Loaf
- Mayonnaise
- Dijon Mustard
- Leftover Turkey Gravy
- Leftover Smoked Turkey
- Shredded White Cheddar Cheese
- Leftover Stuffing
- Cranberry Sauce

Instructions:

- Slice French bread loaf in half and toast on the grill if desired. Spread mayonnaise and Dijon mustard on both halves of the bread.
- Mix to combine leftover smoked turkey and gravy. Layer on top of one bread half.
- Layer remaining **Ingredients** in this order: shredded white cheddar cheese, stuffing and cranberry sauce.
- Top sandwich with other bread half. Slice in half to serve. Enjoy!

5.29 Baked Thanksgiving Shepherd's Pie
Ingredients:

- 1lb Ground Beef
- 2 Cups Leftover Mashed Potatoes
- 1 Cup Leftover Green Beans
- 1 Cup Leftover Stuffing
- 1 Cup Leftover Gravy
- 1 1/2 Lb. Leftover Turkey
- 2 Tbsp Canola Oil
- 1 Cup Chopped Onions
- 2 Cloves Garlic, Minced
- 1 Tsp Kosher Salt
- 1/2 Tsp Freshly Ground Black Pepper
- 2 Tbsp All-Purpose Flour
- 2 Tsp Tomato Paste
- 1 Cup Chicken Broth
- 1 Tsp Worcestershire Sauce
- 2 Tsp Freshly Chopped Rosemary Leaves
- 1 Tsp Freshly Chopped Thyme

Instructions:

- When ready to cook, set temperature to High and preheat, lid closed for 15 minutes.
- Place canola oil in a medium sauté pan over medium-high heat. Once the oil shimmers, add the onion and sauté just until softened and lightly brown, about 3-4 minutes. Add the garlic and stir to combine.
- Add the beef, salt and pepper and cook until browned and cooked through, approximately 3 minutes.
- Sprinkle the onions with the flour and toss to coat, continuing to cook for another minute. Add the tomato paste, leftover gravy, chicken broth, Worcestershire, rosemary and thyme. Stir to combine.
- Bring to a boil, then reduce the heat to low. Cover and simmer 10-12 minutes or until the sauce is thickened slightly.
- Add the leftover turkey, green beans and stuffing to the mixture and spread evenly into an 11 x 7-inch glass baking dish.
- Top with the mashed potatoes, starting around the edges to create a seal to prevent the mixture from bubbling up and smooth with a rubber spatula.
- Place directly on the grill grate and bake for 25 minutes or just until the potatoes begin to brown. Remove to a cooling rack for at least 15 minutes before serving. Enjoy!

5.30 Roasted Cornish Game Stuffed Hens
Ingredients:

- 2 Tbsp Butter
- 1 Pint Wild Mushrooms, Cleaned
- 1/2 Yellow Onion, Diced
- 1 Stalk Celery, Diced
- 1 Clove Garlic, Minced
- 1 Cup Wild Rice
- 1 1/2 Cups Chicken Stock
- 2 Sprigs Thyme, Leaves Removed
- Salt & Pepper as Needed
- 1/2 Tbsp Fresh Sage, Minced
- 4 Cornish Game Hens
- 1/4 Cup Traeger Fin & Feather Rub

Instructions:

- Melt butter in a medium sauce pan and add wild mushrooms. Cook for 10 minutes until softened and lightly browned.
- Add onion and celery and cook 5 minutes until translucent. Add garlic and cook 30 seconds more until fragrant.
- Add rice and stock and bring to a simmer. Cook for about 20 minutes or until rice is tender. Add herbs and season with salt and pepper.
- Stuff 1/4 to 1/2 cup of rice mixture into each bird truss the legs together. Season the exterior of the Cornish game hens liberally with rub.
- When ready to cook, set temperature to 375°F and preheat, lid closed for 15 minutes.
- Place the birds directly on the grill grate and cook for 30 minutes or until the internal temperature registers 165°F with an instant read thermometer.
- Remove from grill and let rest for a few minutes before serving. Enjoy!

5.31 Baked Chicken Pot Pie
Ingredients:

- 2 Tbsp Butter
- 1 Small Yellow Onion, Diced
- 1 Stalk Celery, Diced
- 2 Tbsp Flour
- 2 Cups Homemade Chicken or Turkey Gravy
- 1/2 Cup Cream or Milk
- 1-1/2 Cups Frozen Peas and Carrots, Thawed
- 2 Tsp Dry Sherry (Optional)
- 1/2 Tsp Traeger Pork & Poultry Rub
- 1/4 Tsp Dried Thyme Leaves
- 3-4 Cups Cooked Skinless Chicken or Turkey Meat, Diced
- Salt and Pepper, To Taste
- Flour, For Dusting as Needed
- 1 Sheet Frozen Puff Pastry
- 1 Egg, Beaten With 1 Tbsp Water

Instructions:

- Melt the butter in a large saucepan over medium heat. Add the onion and celery and cook 3 to 5 minutes, or until the onion is translucent. Sprinkle with flour and stir to coat.
- Slowly stream in the chicken stock whisking out any lumps. Add milk or cream and bring to a simmer. Let simmer for a few minutes until slightly thickened, the mixture should coat the back of the spoon. Add the peas and carrots, sherry, Pork and Poultry Rub, thyme leaves, and chicken and simmer for 5 to 10 minutes.
- Coat cast iron skillet with cooking spray and fill with the pot pie filling.
- Unroll the puff pastry sheet on a lightly floured countertop. Let thaw slightly.
- Cover the top of the cast iron with the puff pastry crimping any overhang. Make several small slits in the center to let the steam escape. Brush lightly with the egg wash.
- Transfer the pot pie to the grill.
- Set the temperature to 400°F and preheat, lid closed for 15 minutes.
- Bake the pot pie for 30 minutes, or until the puff pastry is nicely browned and the filling is bubbling. Serve immediately. Enjoy!

5.32 Grilled Chicken Fajitas
Ingredients:

- Cast Iron Fajita Plate
- 2 Ea. Boneless Skinless Chicken Breasts
- 1/2 Tbsp Cumin
- 1/2 Tbsp Chili Powder
- Juice Of 1 Lime
- Salt and Pepper, To Taste
- 1 Small Yellow Onion, Sliced
- 1 Green Bell Pepper, Sliced
- 1 Red Bell Pepper, Sliced
- 1 Tbsp Olive Oil
- Tortillas, To Serve

Instructions:

- Place chicken breasts in a Ziploc bag and add cumin, chili powder, lime juice and salt and pepper. Transfer to the refrigerator and marinate for 1 hour.
- When ready to cook, set temperature to High and preheat, lid closed for 15 minutes.
- Place fajita skillet directly on the grill grate and preheat for 30 minutes. Place olive oil in the pan and add the onions and peppers, season with salt and pepper and close the lid.
- Cook 10 minutes or until lightly browned and cooked through.
- Lay the chicken breast directly on the grill grate next to the skillet and cook 10-15 minutes flipping halfway through until the internal temperature reaches 165°F.

- Remove chicken breast from grill and let rest before slicing.
- Serve sliced chicken with peppers and onions on the fajita plate with tortillas and choice of toppings. Enjoy!

5.33 Smoked Chicken with Chimichurri
Ingredients:

- Chicken Legs
- 6 Whole Bone-In Chicken Legs
- 2 Tbsp Olive Oil
- 1 Tbsp Paprika
- 1 Tbsp Coriander Seeds, Crushed in A Mortar and Pestle
- Zest Of 1 Lime
- 1 1/2 Tsp Sea Salt
- 1 Tsp Freshly Cracked Black Pepper
- 1-2 Limes, Halved, For Serving
- Chimichurri
- 1 Cup Fresh Flat-Leaf Parsley Leaves
- 1 Cup Fresh Cilantro Leaves
- 1 Jalapeño, Halved and Seeds Removed
- 1/2 Medium Spanish Onion, Finely Diced
- 3 Cloves Garlic, Peeled
- 3 Tbsp Fresh Squeezed Lime Juice
- 2 Tbsp Red Wine Vinegar
- 1/3 Cup Extra Virgin Olive Oil
- 1/2 Tsp Sea Salt
- 1/2 Tsp Freshly Cracked Black Pepper

Instructions:

- In a large bowl, massage the chicken legs with the olive oil, paprika, coriander, lime zest, salt, and pepper. For maximum delicious, cover and marinade in the fridge overnight.
- When ready to cook, set the temperature to 425°F and preheat lid closed, for 15 minutes.
- Put the chicken directly on the grill grate, skin side up. Cook for 40-45 minutes or until chicken reads 165°F on an instant-read thermometer.
- *Note: This chimichurri recipe makes extra leftover goodness. Perfect for grilled steak, fish, sandwiches, you name it.
- To make the Chimichurri: Combine all **Ingredients** in the base of a food processor and pulse until smooth & creamy.
- Serve grilled chicken legs with the chimichurri, an extra squeeze of fresh lime juice and your favorite side dish. Enjoy!

5.34 Grilled Sriracha Wings
Ingredients:

- Sweet & Spicy Sriracha Wings
- 2 Tbsp Traeger Chicken Rub
- 2 Tsp Garlic Powder
- 1 Tbsp Sesame Oil
- 2 Lbs. Thawed of Fresh Chicken Wings
- Sauce
- 5 Tbsp Butter, Melted
- 1/3 Cup Dark Brown Sugar
- 1/4 Cup Sriracha
- 2 Tbsp Soy Sauce
- 2 Tbsp Lime Zest
- 1 Tbsp Garlic, Crushed
- 1 Tbsp Ginger, Crushed
- 1 Tbsp Cilantro, Chopped
- 1 Tbsp Toasted Sesame Seeds
- 1 Tbsp Juice from Limes

Instructions:

- When ready to cook, set the Traeger to 325°F and preheat, lid closed for 15 minutes.
- Combine Traeger Chicken rub, garlic powder, sesame oil, and wings. Toss to coat.

- Place the wings directly on the grill grate and cook for 25 to 30 minutes, or until the chicken reaches an internal temperature of 160°F.
- While wings are cooking, combine all the sauce **Ingredients** except for the cilantro and sesame seeds.
- Once wings reach an internal temperature of 160°F, remove from grill and increase the grill temperature to High.
- While grill heats, toss the cooked wings in half of the sauce mixture (just enough to coat them) and place back on the grill for 10 to 15 minutes, or until sauce sets.
- Top wings with chopped cilantro and sesame seeds and serve with the remaining sauce on the side. Enjoy!

5.35 Whole Smoked Chicken
Ingredients:

- Brine
- 1/2 Cup Kosher Salt
- 1 Cup Brown Sugar
- 1 Gallon Water
- Whole Chicken
- Traeger Big Game Rub
- 1 Tsp Garlic, Minced
- 1 (3 To 3 1/2 Lb.) Whole Chicken
- 1 Lemon, Halved
- 1 Medium Yellow Onion, Quartered
- 3 Whole Garlic Cloves
- 4-5 Sprigs Thyme

Instructions:

- For the Brine: Dissolve the kosher salt and brown sugar in 1 gallon of water. Once dissolved, place the chicken in the brine and refrigerate overnight. Make sure chicken is fully submerged weighing it down if necessary.
- When ready to cook, set the Traeger to 225°F and preheat, lid closed for 15 minutes.
- While the grill preheats, remove the chicken from the brine and pat dry. Rub with the minced garlic and Big Game rub.
- Next, stuff the cavity with the lemon, onion, garlic and thyme. Tie the legs together.
- Place chicken directly on the grill grate and smoke for 2-1/2 to 3 hours or until an instant read thermometer reads 160°F when inserted into the thickest part of the breast.
- The finished internal temperature will rise to 165°F in the breast as the chicken rests. Enjoy!

5.36 Grilled Honey Garlic Wings
Ingredients:

- 2-1/2 Lbs. Chicken Wings
- Traeger Pork & Poultry Rub, As Needed
- 4 Tbsp Butter
- 1/2 Cup Hot Sauce
- 1/4 Cup Honey
- 2-3 Cloves Minced Garlic
- 1 1/2 Cups Blue Cheese or Ranch Dressing

Instructions:

- Start by segmenting the wings into three pieces, cutting through the joints. Discard the wing tips or save them to make a stock.
- Lay out the remaining pieces on a rimmed baking sheet lined with nonstick foil or parchment paper. Season well with Traeger Pork and Poultry rub.
- When ready to cook, set temperature to 350°F and preheat, lid closed for 15 minutes.
- Place the baking sheet with wings directly on the grill grate and cook for 45-50 minutes or until they are no longer pink at the bone.
- To make the sauce: Melt butter in a small saucepan. Add the garlic and sauté for 2-3 minutes. Add in the honey and hot sauce and cook for a few minutes until completely combined.
- Keep sauce warm while the wings are cooking. When wings are done, pour the spicy honey-garlic sauce over the wings, turning with tongs to coat.
- Place wings back on the grill and cook for an additional 10-15 minutes to set the sauce5.37 Roasted Beer Can Chicken

Ingredients:

- 1 (3-5 Lb.) Whole Chicken
- Traeger Chicken Rub, As Needed
- 1 Can Beer

Instructions:

- Tuck the wing tips back and truss the chicken legs together.
- Season chicken generously with Traeger Chicken Rub, including the cavity.
- Open the can of beer and set the chicken on top of the beer. Make sure all but the bottom 1-1/2" of the beer can is in the cavity of the chicken.
- When ready to cook, set the Traeger to 350°F and preheat, lid closed for 15 minutes.
- Place chicken on a sheet tray and place directly on the grill grate. Cook for 60-75 minutes or until the internal temperature registers 165°F in the thickest part of the breast.
- Remove from the grill and let rest 5-10 minutes before carving. Enjoy!

5.38 Competition BBQ Chicken Thighs
Ingredients:

- 20 Bone in Chicken Thighs (Approximately 1/2 Lb. Each)
- 3 Sticks Melted Butter
- 6 Oz Traeger Big Game Rub
- 20 Oz Low Sodium Chicken Broth
- 24 Oz Traeger Apricot BBQ Sauce

Instructions:

- Peel skin off the thighs. With kitchen shears remove the fat on each side of the chicken thighs.
- Trim 1/4" off the bottom and top bone knuckle of the chicken thighs. Trim so that the thighs are uniform in size.
- Trim skin to fit now trimmed thighs. Place the skin back on the thighs.
- Once done with all thighs, inject 1/2 oz of low sodium chicken broth into each side of the thigh and let rest for 60 minutes.
- While resting, season the top of the chicken thighs with Traeger Big Game Rub. Place in a refrigerator or cold cooler until ready to cook.
- Place thighs in a large disposable pan and add the melted butter to the pan as a braising liquid.
- When ready to cook, set temperature to 250°F and preheat, lid closed for 15 minutes.
- Slide the whole disposable pan of chicken on the grate and cook for one hour. After one hour, wrap the top of the disposable pan in aluminum foil and cook for another hour or until the internal temperature reaches 165°F.
- Once thighs reach internal temperature of 165°F, use tongs to remove each chicken thigh and dunk it into heated Traeger Apricot BBQ sauce.
- Place back in a clean disposable pan and cook for an additional 20 minutes. Remove from grill and let rest for 10 minutes before serving. Enjoy!

5.39 Roasted Sweet Thai Chili Wings
Ingredients:

- Wings
- 3 To 4 Lbs. Chicken Wings, Drumettes And Flappers Preferred, Separated Over the Entire Wing
- Meat Church Holy Gospel Seasoning, As Needed
- Toasted Sesame Seeds, To Garnish
- Sliced Green Onions, To Garnish
- Sweet Thai Chili Sauce
- 1/2 Cup Sugar
- 1/2 Cup Rice Vinegar
- 1/4 Cup Water
- 3 Tbsp Fish Sauce
- 2 Tbsp Cooking Sherry
- 4 Cloves Garlic, Minced Fine
- 1/2 Tbsp To 1 Tbsp Dried Crushed Chili Pepper, Depending on Desired Heat Level
- 1 1/2 Tbsp Cornstarch, Dissolved In 4 Tbsp Water

Instructions:

- For the Thai Chili Sauce: Place all **Ingredients** except the cornstarch in a sauce pan and whisk to combine. Bring the mixture to a slight boil and simmer for 10 minutes. Reduce heat and add the cornstarch and water mixture. Stir until thickened, about 2-3 minutes. Remove sauce from heat while wings cook.
- When ready to cook, set temperature to High and preheat, lid closed for 15 minutes.
- This temperature will help get the wings crisper than a lower temperature cooks which can lead to rubbery skin.
- If you bought the whole wing, remove the tip and separate the drumette and wing from each other. Pat them dry. Season the wings moderately on all sides with Meat Church Holy Gospel Rub. This is a blend of our Holy Cow and our Gospel All-Purpose rubs. It is amazing as the base for chicken.
- Place wings directly on the grill grate and cook for a total time of 20 minutes. Flip the wings halfway through the cook. I like to get as many tasty bites of char on my wings and flipping them will help achieve this on an additional side.
- Using an instant thermometer to test the internal temperature of chicken wings. The finished temperature should be between 165 -180°F after about 20 minutes. While chicken is safe to eat at 165°F, it is ok to take wings even further as it is difficult to dry them out.
- To finish the wings, toss wings in the sweet Thai chili sauce. Place them back on Traeger for 5 minutes to allow sauce to set. This will prevent the sauce from running all over you when trying to eat.
- Remove and allow to cool slightly. Enjoy!

5.40 BBQ Chicken Thighs
Ingredients:

- 6 Bone-In Chicken Thighs, Skin On
- Traeger Big Game Rub
- Salt and Ground Black Pepper, To Taste

Instructions:

- When ready to cook, set the Traeger to 350°F and preheat, lid closed for 15 minutes.
- While grill is heating, trim excess fat and skin from chicken thighs. Season with a light layer of salt and pepper and a layer of Traeger Big Game rub.
- Place chicken thighs on the grill grate and cook for 35 minutes. Check internal temperature, chicken is done at 165°F, but there is enough fat that they will stay moist at an internal temperature of 180°F and the texture is better.
- Remove from the grill and let rest for 5 minutes before serving. Enjoy!

5.41 Smoked Chicken Leg & Thigh Quarters
Ingredients:

- 8 Connected Chicken Leg and Thigh Pieces
- 3 Tbsp Olive Oil
- Traeger Pork & Poultry Rub, To Taste

Instructions:

- Rinse the chicken pieces under cold running water and pat dry with paper towels.
- Place the chicken pieces in a large mixing bowl. Pour oil over the chicken to coat each piece, then season to taste with the rub. Massage the chicken pieces to encourage the oil and seasonings get under the skin.
- Cover and refrigerate for at least 1 to 2 hours.
- When ready to cook, set temperature to 180°F and preheat, lid closed for 15 minutes.
- Remove the chicken from the refrigerator, letting any excess oil drip back into the bowl. Arrange the chicken on the grill grate and smoke for 1 hour.
- Increase grill temperature to 350°F and continue to roast the chicken until the internal temperature in the thickest part of a thigh is 165°F, or the chicken is golden brown and the juices run clear, about 50 to 60 minutes.
- Allow the chicken to rest for 8-10 minutes and serve. Enjoy!

5.42 Smoked Wings
Ingredients:

- 24 Wings (Sectioned)
- 12 Oz Italian Dressing
- 3 Oz Traeger Chicken Rub
- 8 Oz Traeger Chili Barbecue Sauce

Instructions:

- Wash all wings and place into resealable bag.
- Add Italian Dressing to the resealable bag containing the wings. Place in refrigerator and allow to marinate for 6-12 hours.
- When ready to cook, set the Traeger to 225°F and preheat, lid closed for 15 minutes.
- Remove wings from marinade and shake off excess marinade. Season all sides of the wings with Traeger Chicken Rub and let sit for 15 minutes before putting wings on the Traeger.
- Cook wings to an internal temperature of 160°F.
- Remove the wings and toss in Chili Barbecue Sauce.
- Increase the temperature to 375°F and preheat. Once at temperature, place the wings on the Traeger and sear both sides getting the internal temperature of the chicken wings to at least 165°F.
- Remove the wings from the smoker and let rest for 5 minutes.
- Serve with your favorite side wing dressing or sauce. Enjoy!

5.43 Chicken Parmesan Sliders with Pesto Mayonnaise
Ingredients:

- 2 Lbs. Ground Chicken
- 1 Cup Parmesan Cheese, Shredded
- 1 Tbsp. Worcestershire Sauce
- A Few Grinds Black Pepper, Freshly Ground
- 1 Cup Mayonnaise
- 2 Tbsp. Prepared Pesto Sauce
- 12 Slider Buns, Split
- 3 Roma Tomatoes, Thinly Sliced
- 1 Small Red Onion, Thinly Sliced
- For Serving Fresh Spinach or Arugula Leaves, Washed, And Dried

Instructions:

- Line a baking sheet with plastic wrap. In a large mixing bowl, combine the ground chicken, the Parmesan, the Worcestershire, and a few grinds of black pepper. Wet your hands with cold water, and use them to mix the **Ingredients.**
- Divide the meat mixture in half, then form six 2-inch patties out of each half. Place the patties on the baking sheet, cover with another sheet of plastic wrap, and refrigerate for at least 1 hour.
- Combine the mayonnaise and pesto in a small bowl and whisk together. Cover and refrigerate until serving time.
- When ready to cook, start the Traeger grill on Smoke with the lid open until the fire is established (4 to 5 minutes). Set the temperature to 300F and preheat, lid closed, for 10 to 15 minutes.
- Arrange the chicken patties on the grill grate and grill, turning once, until the patties are cooked through (165F), about 30 minutes.
- To serve, put a chicken patty on the bottom of a slider bun and top with a dollop of the pesto mayonnaise. Add tomato, onion, and spinach as desired. Replace the top of the bun and skewer with a frilled toothpick, if desired.

5.44 Chicken Picadillo Empanadas
Ingredients:

- 1 Lb. Chicken, Shredded
- 2 Carrots
- 2 Stalks Celery
- 1 Tbsp Vegetable Oil
- Salt and Pepper
- 1/4 Cup Water
- 1 Tsp Chicken Bouillon
- 1 Small Can Tomato Juice
- 1 Egg, Scrambled
- 2 Rolls Pie Crust
- 1 Large Oven Safe Pan

Instructions:

- Start the Traeger on Smoke with the lid open until a fire is established (4-5 minutes). Then turn temperature to 450 degrees F and preheat, lid closed, for 10 to 15 minutes.
- Chop carrots and celery. Set a large oven safe skillet into your Traeger, heat oil in skillet and cook carrots and celery. Add salt and pepper. Cook until carrots and celery soften, about 5 to 10 minutes, stirring occasionally.
- Once vegetables soften, add chicken, tomato juice, water and chicken bouillon. Cook an additional 5-10 minutes or until sauce starts to thicken.
- Turn the heat down to 350 degrees F.
- Roll out pie crusts and cut circles about 4" in diameter.
- Place some filling in the middle of the dough and rub a little egg wash on one half of the circle's edge. This will ensure a good seal when you fold it over and press.
- Fold dough over and press to make half-moon pastries.
- Brush the top of the pastries with a little egg wash and a dash of salt. Transfer them to the grill.
- Grill for 10-15 minutes at 350 degrees F. When golden brown, serve with cilantro lime sour cream! Enjoy!

5.45 Chicken Salad
Ingredients:

- 1 Qt. Cold Water
- 1/4 Cup Kosher Salt
- 4 Large Chicken Breasts, Boneless
- 4 Chicken Thighs, Bone-In
- 1/2 Red Bell Pepper, Finely Diced
- 1/2 Green Bell, Finely Diced
- 2 Scallions, Thinly Sliced
- 1 To 2 Tbsp. Pickled Jalapeno Peppers, Minced
- 1 Cup Mayonnaise
- 1 Tbsp. Fresh Lime Juice
- 1 Tsp. Ground Cumin
- 1 Tsp. Black Pepper, Freshly Ground
- 1/2 Tsp. Garlic Salt
- 2 Tbsp. Fresh Cilantro Leaves, Minced

Instructions:

- For the brine, in a large saucepan or mixing bowl, combine the water and salt and stir until the salt crystals dissolve. Add the chicken breasts and thighs. Cover and refrigerate for 2 to 4 hours.
- Drain, but do not dry the chicken: Smoke clings better to wet surfaces.
- When ready to cook, start the Traeger grill on Smoke with the lid open until the fire is established (4 to 5 minutes).
- Arrange the chicken on the grill grate and smoke for 30 minutes. Increase the temperature to 350F and continue to cook the chicken until the juices run clear and the internal temperature when read on an instant-read meat thermometer is 165F, 25 to 30 minutes.
- Transfer to a cutting board and let cool. Dice the chicken, discarding any skin, bones, or gobbets of fat.

- Transfer to a mixing bowl. Add the red and green bell peppers, the scallions, and pickled jalapenos. Stir gently to distribute the **Ingredients** set aside.
- In a mixing bowl, whisk together the mayonnaise, lime juice, cumin, black pepper, and garlic salt. Stir in the cilantro.
- Add the dressing to the chicken mixture and stir gently until well-combined.
- Transfer to a serving bowl. Dust with paprika. Serve immediately, or cover and chill for up to 3 days. Enjoy!

Chapter 6: Turkey Recipes

6.1 Herb Roasted Turkey
Ingredients:

- 8 Tbsp. Butter, Room Temperature
- 2 Tbsp. Mixed Herbs Such as Parsley, Sage, Rosemary, And Marjoram, Chopped
- 1/4 Tsp. Black Pepper, Freshly Ground
- 1 (12-14 Lbs.) Turkey, Thawed If Previously Frozen
- 3 Tbsp. Butter
- As Needed Traeger Pork and Poultry Rub
- 2 Cups Chicken or Turkey Broth

Instructions:

- In a small mixing bowl, combine the 8 tablespoons of softened butter, mixed herbs, and black pepper and beat until fluffy with a wooden spoon. (You can make the herbed butter several days ahead: Cover and refrigerate, but bring to room temperature before using).
- Remove any giblets from the turkey cavity and save them for gravy making, if desired. Wash the turkey, inside and out, under cold running water. Dry with paper towels. Place the turkey on a roasting rack in a roasting pan. Tuck the wings behind the back, and tie the legs together with butcher's string.
- Using your fingers or the handle of a wooden spoon, gently push some of the herbed butter underneath the turkey skin onto the breast halves, being careful not to tear the skin. Massage the skin to evenly distribute the herbed butter.
- Rub the outside of the turkey with the melted butter and sprinkle with the Traeger Pork and Poultry Rub. Pour the chicken broth in the bottom of the roasting pan.
- When ready to cook, set temperature to 325°F and preheat, lid closed for 15 minutes.
- Put the roasting pan with the turkey directly on the grill grate. Roast the turkey for 3 hours. Insert the probe from the meat thermometer in the thickest part of the thigh, but not touching bone. Cook until internal temperature reaches 165°F. The turkey should also be beautifully browned with crisp skin. If the temperature is less than that, or if your turkey is not browned to your liking, let it roast for another 30 minutes, then check the temperature again. Repeat until the turkey is fully cooked.
- When the turkey is done, carefully transfer it to a cutting board and let it rest for 20 to 30 minutes. Do not tent it with aluminum foil or the skin will lose its crispness. Use the drippings that have accumulated in the bottom of the roasting pan to make gravy, if desired. Carve the turkey and serve.

6.2 Smoked Bourbon & Orange Brined Turkey
Ingredients:

- Traeger Orange Brine (From Kit)
- Traeger Turkey Rub (From Kit)
- 1.25-2.5 Gallons Cold Water
- 1 Cup Bourbon
- 1 Tbsp. Butter, Melted
- 1 Tbsp. Grand Marnier Or Other Orange-Flavored Liquor

Instructions:

- Mix Traeger Orange Brine seasoning (from Orange Brine & Turkey Rub Kit) with one quart of water. Boil for 5 minutes. Remove from heat, add 1 gallon of cold water and bourbon. Refrigerate until completely cooled.
- Place turkey breast side down in a large container. Pour cooled brine mix over bird. Add cold water until bird is submerged. Refrigerate for 24 hours.
- Remove turkey and disregard brine. Blot turkey dry with paper towels. Combine butter and Grand Marnier and coat outside of turkey.
- Season outside of turkey with Traeger Turkey Rub (from Orange Brine & Turkey Rub Kit).
- When ready to cook, set temperature to 225°F and preheat, lid closed for 15 minutes.
- Smoke turkey, breast up, for 2 hours. Increase temperature to 350°F and roast turkey until the internal temperature of the thickest part of the high reaches 165F, 2 to 3 hours, depending on size of turkey.
- Let rest 20 to 30 minutes before serving. Enjoy!

6.3 Traeger Leftover Turkey Soup
Ingredients:

- 1 Turkey Carcass
- 16 Cups Cold Water
- 2 Large Celery Ribs, Sliced
- 2 Large Carrots, Scraped and Sliced
- 2 Red Onions, Quartered
- 10 Sprigs Fresh Flat Parsley Leaf
- 1 Tbsp. Peppercorn
- 2 Tsp. Fresh Thyme

Instructions:

- Strip a turkey carcass of all meat; set aside in a container.
- Break up the bones of the turkey carcass and place them in a large pot. Add any turkey skin or other assorted "bits" that are not edible meat. For the best taste, make the stock the day after the turkey has been cooked. Pour in the cold water and turn heat to high; bring to a boil.
- Once the stock has come to a boil, add all remaining **Ingredients** and turn heat down until the bubbles barely break the surface. Let simmer for 3 to 4 hours, stirring occasionally. The broth tastes best when reduced to 7 or 8 cups of stock.
- When the stock is ready, strain it through a fine-meshed sieve into a large bowl; if your sieve is not fine, line it first with cheesecloth. Discard the bones and veggies you used to make the stock (all their flavor is now in the stock).
- Refrigerate stock, covered, for several hours or preferably overnight. You can either make soup the next day, or freeze the stock; make sure you skim off the solidified fat before you either make soup or freeze the stock.
- When ready to make the actual soup, heat up the homemade stock on the stovetop. Dish stock into individual bowls. Add shredded turkey, desired vegetables (such as chopped celery and red onions), fresh herbs (such as rosemary and thyme) and freshly ground pepper.

6.4 Smoked Turkey
Ingredients:

- Smoked Turkey by Rob cooks
- 1 (12-14 Lb.) Turkey, Fresh or Thawed
- 3/4 Lb. (3 Sticks) Unsalted Butter
- 1 (5 Gal) Bucket or Stock Pot
- Foil Pan, Large Enough for Turkey
- Heavy Duty Foil
- Brine
- 2 Cups Kosher Salt
- 2 Cups Sugar
- 2-Gals (1/2 Gal Is Ice) Water
- Rub
- 1/2 Cup Kosher Salt
- 1/2 Cup Coarse Ground Black Pepper

Instructions:

- This method requires an overnight brining so collect everything the day before your meal.
- The afternoon before, prepare your brine by adding the kosher salt and sugar to a medium saucepan. Cover with water and bring to a boil. Stir to dissolve the salt and sugar. Pour salt and sugar concentrate into a bucket, add ice and water up to 2 gallons.
- Prepare your turkey by removing the neck, gizzards and truss, if pre-trussed. Trim off excess skin and fat near the cavity and neck. Place the turkey in bucket with the brine. If it floats, place a plate or two on top to keep the turkey submerged. Cover bucket and place in fridge until ready to cook the next afternoon.
- When ready to cook, set temperature to 180°F and preheat, lid closed for 15 minutes.
- Remove your turkey from the brine. Remember there's a cavity full of water so make sure to do this over the sink, otherwise you'll have brine all over the place. Set your turkey down on a cookie sheet to prepare it for the smoker.
- Mix up the kosher salt and pepper in a shaker, sprinkle the rub on all parts of the turkey, don't sprinkle inside the cavity! There is no need to tie up the legs and wings with this method. The fan in the Traeger pushes air all around the turkey during the cook.
- Put the turkey on the grill at 180°F for 2 hours, 225°F for the next hour, and finally 325°F to finish it off. Place it so the legs and thighs are towards the hotter area of your smoker and the breast to the cooler side. Check the turkey after a couple hours for color. When it reaches your desired color place it in the foil pan.
- Cut the butter up into squares and pile them on the turkey.
- Wrap in heavy-duty foil and put it back on the smoker. Cook until temperature in the breast reaches 165°F and the thigh reaches 180°F.
- Remove from smoker and allow it to rest for 30 minutes before carving.

6.5 Smoked Turkey Legs
Ingredients:

- 1 Gal Warm Water
- 1/2-Gal Cold Water
- 4 Cups Ice
- 1 Cup Traeger BBQ Rub
- 1/2 Cup Curing Salt
- 1/2 Cup Brown Sugar
- 1 Tbsp Allspice Berries, Crushed (Optional)
- 1 Tbsp Whole Black Peppercorns
- 2 Bay Leaves
- 2 Tsp Liquid Smoke
- 4 Turkey Legs

Instructions:

- In a large stockpot, combine one gallon of warm water, the rub, curing salt, brown sugar, allspice (if using), peppercorns, bay leaves and liquid smoke.
- Bring to a boil over high heat to dissolve the salt granules. Cool to room temperature.

- Add cold water and ice; chill in the refrigerator. Add the turkey legs, making sure they're completely submerged in the brine.
- After 24 hours, drain the turkey legs and discard the brine. Rinse the brine off the legs with cold water, then dry thoroughly with paper towels. Brush off any clinging solid spices.
- When ready to cook, set temperature to 250°F and preheat, lid closed for 15 minutes.
- Lay the turkey legs directly on the grill grate. Smoke for 4-5 hours, or until the internal temperature reaches 165°F on an instant-read meat thermometer. Make sure the probe doesn't touch bone or you'll get a false reading.
- The turkey legs should be deeply browned. Don't be alarmed if the meat under the skin is pinkish: That's a chemical reaction to the cure and the smoke.
- Serve immediately. Enjoy!

6.6 Traditional Thanksgiving Turkey
Ingredients:

- 1 (18-20lb) Turkey
- 1/2 Lb. Butter, Softened
- 8 Sprigs Thyme
- 6 Cloves Garlic, Minced
- 1 Sprig Rosemary, Rough Chop
- 1 Tbsp Cracked Black Pepper
- 1/2 Tbsp Kosher Salt

Instructions:

- In a small bowl, combine butter with the minced garlic, thyme leaves, chopped rosemary, black pepper and kosher salt.
- Prepare the turkey by separating the skin from the breast creating a pocket to stuff the butter-herb mixture in.
- Cover the entire breast with 1/4" thickness of butter mixture.
- Season the whole turkey with kosher salt and black pepper. As an option, you can also stuff the turkey cavity with Traditional Stuffing.
- When ready to cook, set the temperature to 300°F and preheat, lid closed for 15 minutes.
- Place turkey on the grill and roast for 3-4 hours. Check the internal temperature, the desired temperature is 175°F in the thigh next to the bone, and 160°F in the breast.
- Turkey will continue to cook once taken off grill to reach a final temperature of 165°F in the breast.
- Let rest for 10-15 minutes before carving. Enjoy!

6.7 Turkey Jalapeno Meatballs
Ingredients:

- Turkey Jalapeño Meatballs
- 1 1/4 Lbs. Ground Turkey
- 1 Jalapeño Pepper, Deseeded and Finely Diced
- 1/2 Tsp Garlic Salt
- 1 Tsp Onion Powder
- 1 Tsp Salt
- 1/2 Tsp Ground Black Pepper
- 1/4 Tsp Worcestershire Sauce
- Cayenne Pepper, Pinch
- 1 Large Egg, Beaten
- 1/4 Cup Milk
- 1/2 Cup Plain Bread Crumbs Or Panko
- Glaze
- 1 Cup Canned Jellied Cranberry Sauce
- 1/2 Cup Orange Marmalade
- 1/2 Cup Chicken Broth
- 1 Tbsp Jalapeño Pepper, Minced
- Salt, To Taste
- Ground Black Pepper, To Taste

Instructions:

- In a separate small bowl, combine the milk and bread crumbs.
- In a large bowl, mix together turkey, garlic salt, onion powder, salt, pepper, Worcestershire sauce, cayenne pepper, egg and jalapeños.
- Add the bread crumb milk mixture to the bowl and combine. Cover with plastic and refrigerate for up to 1 hour.
- When ready to cook, set the temperature to 350°F and preheat, lid closed for 15 minutes
- Roll the turkey mixture into balls, about one tablespoon each and place the meatballs in a single layer on a parchment lined baking sheet.
- Cook meatballs until they start to brown, flipping occasionally until they reach an internal temperature of 175 degrees F and all sides are browned (about 20 minutes).
- Glaze: Combine cranberry sauce, marmalade, chicken broth, and jalapeños and cook over medium heat in a small saucepan on the stovetop. Cook until **Ingredients:** are incorporated.
- Half way through meatball cook time, brush the meatballs with the cranberry glaze.
- Transfer meatballs to a serving dish with cranberry glaze on the side. Serve immediately. Enjoy!

6.8 Wild Turkey Southwest Egg Rolls
Ingredients:

- 2 Cups Leftover Wild Turkey Meat
- 1/2 Cup Corn
- 1/2 Cup Black Beans
- 3 Tbsp Taco Seasoning
- 1/2 Cup White Onion, Chopped
- 4 Cloves Garlic, Minced
- 1 Poblano Pepper (Or 2 Jalapeño Peppers), Chopped
- 1 Can Rote Tomatoes & Chiles
- 1/2 Cup Water
- 12 Egg Roll Wrappers

Instructions:

- Add olive oil to a large skillet and heat on the stove over medium heat. Add onions and peppers and sauté 2-3 minutes until soft. Add garlic, cook 30 seconds, then Rote and black beans. Reduce heat and simmer.
- Pour taco seasoning over meat and add 1/3 cup of water and mix to coat well. Add to veggie mixture and stir to mix well. If it seems dry, add 2 tbsp water. Cook until heated all the way through.
- Remove from the heat and transfer the mixture to the fridge. The mixture should be completely cooled prior to stuffing the egg rolls or the wrappers will break.
- Place spoonful of the mixture in each wrapper and wrap tightly. Repeat with remaining wrappers. When ready to cook, set temperature to High and preheat, lid closed for 15 minutes.
- Brush each egg roll with oil or butter and place directly on the Traeger grill grate. Cook until the exterior is crispy, about 20 min per side.
- Remove from Traeger and cool. Serve. Enjoy!

6.9 Smoked Wild Turkey Breast
Ingredients:

- Brine
- 2 Lbs. Turkey Breast and Deboned Thigh, Tied with Skin On
- 1 Cup Brown Sugar
- 1/4 Cup Salt
- 2 Tbsp Cracked Pepper
- 4 Cups Cold Water
- BBQ Rub
- 2 Tbsp Garlic Powder
- 2 Tbsp Onions, Dried
- 2 Tbsp Black Pepper
- 2 Tbsp Brown Sugar
- 1 Tbsp Cayenne Pepper
- 2 Tbsp Chili Powder
- 1/4 Cup Paprika
- 1 Tbsp Salt
- 2 Tbsp Sugar
- 2 Tbsp Cumin, Ground

Instructions:

- For the Brine: In a large glass bowl combine brown sugar, salt, pepper and water. Add turkey and weigh down to completely submerge if necessary. Transfer to the refrigerator and brine for 12-24 hours.
- Remove turkey from the brine and discard the brine.
- When ready to cook, set the temperature 180°F and preheat lid closed for 15 minutes.
- Combine **Ingredients** for the BBQ Rub. Season turkey with rub and place directly on the grill grate skin side up.
- Smoke for 5-8 hours or until the internal temperature reaches 160°F degrees when an instant read thermometer is inserted into the center.
- Remove from the smoker and let rest for 10 minutes. Turkey will continue to cook once taken off grill to reach a final temperature of 165°F in the breast.
- Slice and serve with your favorite sides. Enjoy!

6.10 Grilled Wild Turkey Orange Cashew Salad
Ingredients:

- Turkey Breast
- 2 Wild Turkey Breast Halves, Without Skin
- 1/4 Cup Teriyaki Sauce
- 1 Tsp Fresh Ginger
- 1 (12 Oz) Can Blood Orange Kill Cliff or Similar Citrus Soda
- 2 Tbsp Traeger Chicken Rub
- Cashew Salad
- 4 Cups Romaine Lettuce, Chopped
- 1/2 Head Red or White Cabbage, Chopped
- 1/2 Cup Shredded Carrots
- 1/2 Cup Edamame, Shelled
- 1 Smoked Yellow Bell Pepper, Sliced into Circles
- 1 Smoked Red Bell Pepper, Sliced into Circles
- 3 Chive Tips, Chopped
- 1/2 Cup Smoked Cashews
- Blood Orange Vinaigrette
- 1 Tsp Orange Zest
- Juice From 1/2 Large Orange
- 1 Tsp Finely Grated Fresh Ginger
- 2 Tbsp Seasoned Rice Vinegar
- 1 Tsp Honey
- 1/4 Cup Light Vegetable Oil

Instructions:

- For the Marinade: Combine teriyaki sauce, Kill Cliff soda and fresh ginger. Pour marinade over turkey breasts in a Ziplock bag or dish and seal. Marinate in the refrigerator for 6 to 24 hours, turning occasionally.
- When ready to cook, set temperature to 375°F and preheat, lid closed for 15 minutes.
- Remove turkey from the refrigerator, drain the marinade and pat turkey dry with paper towels.
- Place turkey into a shallow oven proof dish and season with Traeger Chicken Rub.
- Place dish in the Traeger and cook for 30-45 minutes or until the breast reaches an internal temperature of 160°F.
- Remove the breast from the grill and wrap in Traeger Butcher Paper. Let turkey rest for 10 minutes. While turkey is resting, prepare salad.
- Assemble salad **Ingredients** in a bowl and toss to mix. Combine all **Ingredients** in list for vinaigrette.
- After resting for 10 minutes, slice turkey and serve with cashew salad and blood orange vinaigrette. Enjoy!

6.11 Baked Cornbread Turkey Tamale Pie
Ingredients:

- Filling
- 2 Cups Shredded Turkey
- 2 Cobs of Corn
- 1 (15 Oz) Can Black Beans, Rinsed and Drained
- 1 Yellow Bell Pepper
- 1 Orange Bell Pepper
- 2 Jalapeños
- 2 Tbsp Cilantro
- 1 Bunch Green Onions
- 1/2 Tsp Cumin
- 1/2 Tsp Paprika
- 1 (7 Oz) Can Chipotle Sauce
- 1 (15 Oz) Can Enchilada Sauce
- 1/2 Cup Shredded Cheddar Cheese
- Cornbread Topping
- 1 Cup All-Purpose Flour
- 1 Cup Yellow or White Cornmeal
- 1 Tbsp Sugar
- 2 Tsp Baking Powder
- 1/2 Tsp Salt
- 3 Tbsp Butter
- 1 Cup Buttermilk
- 1 Large Egg, Lightly Beaten

Instructions:

- For the filling: Mix to combine filling **Ingredients** Place in the bottom of a butter greased 10-inch pan.
- For the cornbread topping: In a mixing bowl, combine the flour, cornmeal, sugar, baking powder, and salt. Melt the butter in a small saucepan. Remove butter from the heat and stir in the milk and egg. Make sure the mixture isn't too hot or the egg will curdle.
- Add the milk-egg mixture to the dry **Ingredients** and stir to combine. Do not over mix.
- To assemble Tamale Pie: Fill the bottom of a butter greased 10-inch pan with the shredded turkey filling. Top with the cornbread topping and smooth to the edges of pan.
- When ready to cook, set the temperature to 375°F and preheat, lid closed for 15 minutes.
- Place directly on the grill grate and cook for 45-50 minutes or until the cornbread is lightly browned and cooked through. Enjoy!

6.12 BBQ Pulled Turkey Sandwiches
Ingredients:

- 6 Turkey Thighs, Skin-On
- 1 1/2 Cups Chicken or Turkey Broth
- Traeger Pork & Poultry Rub
- 1 Cup Traeger BBQ Sauce, Or More as Needed
- 6 Buns or Kaiser Rolls, Split and Buttered

Instructions:

- Season turkey thighs on both sides with the Traeger Pork & Poultry rub.
- When ready to cook, set temperature to 180°F and preheat, lid closed for 15 minutes.
- Arrange the turkey thighs directly on the grill grate and smoke for 30 minutes.
- Transfer the thighs to a sturdy disposable aluminum foil or roasting pan. Pour the broth around the thighs. Cover the pan with foil or a lid.
- Increase temperature to 325°F and preheat, lid closed. Roast the thighs until they reach an internal temperature of 180°F.
- Remove pan from the grill, but leave grill on. Let the turkey thighs cool slightly until they can be comfortably handled.
- Pour off the drippings and reserve. Remove the skin and discard.
- Pull the turkey meat into shreds with your fingers and return the meat to the roasting pan.
- Add 1 cup or more of your favorite Traeger BBQ Sauce along with some of the drippings.
- Recover the pan with foil and reheat the BBQ turkey on the Traeger for 20 to 30 minutes.
- Serve with toasted buns if desired. Enjoy!

6.13 Roasted Spatchcock Turkey
Ingredients:

- 1 (18-20 Lb.) Whole Turkey
- 4 Tbsp Traeger Turkey Rub
- 1 Tbsp Jacobsen Sea Salt
- 4 Cloves Garlic, Minced
- 3 Tbsp Parsley, Chopped
- 1 Tbsp Rosemary, Chopped
- 2 Tbsp Thyme Leaves, Chopped
- 2 Scallions, Chopped
- 3 Tbsp Olive Oil

Instructions:

- When ready to cook, set temperature to High and preheat, lid closed for 15 minutes.
- On a cutting board, combine garlic, parsley, thyme, rosemary, and scallions. Chop together until the mixture forms a paste. Set aside.
- To spatchcock the turkey: With a large knife or shears, cut the bird open along the backbone on both sides, through the ribs and remove the backbone.
- Once the bird is open, split the breastbone to spread the bird flat; this will allow it to roast evenly.
- With the bird breast side up, season the exterior with half the Traeger Turkey Rub then follow with 2/3 the herb mixture rubbing it into the bird. Drizzle with olive oil.
- Flip the bird and season generously with the remaining Traeger Turkey Rub.
- Place the turkey directly on the grill grate and cook for 30 minutes.
- Reduce the temperature on the grill to 300°F and continue to cook for 3-4 hours or until the internal temperature reaches 160°F in the breast.
- The finished internal temperature should reach 165°F, but the temperature will continue to rise after the bird is removed from the grill.
- Let the bird rest 20-25 minutes before carving. Enjoy!

6.14 Spatchcocked Maple Brined Turkey
Ingredients:

- 1 (12-14 Lbs.) Turkey, Thawed If Frozen
- 5 Qtrs. Hot Water
- 1 1/2 Cups Kosher Salt
- 3/4 Cup Bourbon
- 1 Cup Pure Maple Syrup
- 1/2 Cup Brown Sugar
- 1 Onion, Peeled and Quartered Through the Root End
- 3 To 4 Strips Orange Peel
- 3 Bay Leaves, Broken into Pieces
- 2 Tbsp Black Peppercorns
- 1 Tbsp Whole Cloves
- 3 Qtrs. Ice
- 1 Cup Butter, Melted
- Traeger Pork & Poultry Rub, As Needed
- Sprigs of Fresh Sage and Thyme, To Garnish
- Orange Wedges, Lady Apples, Or Kumquats, To Serve

Instructions:

- Note: Do not use a kosher turkey or a self-basting turkey for this recipe as they have already been enhanced with a salt-solution.
- For the Brine: In a large stockpot or container, combine the hot water, kosher salt, bourbon, 3/4 cup of the maple syrup, brown sugar, onion, bay leaves, orange peel, peppercorns, and cloves and stir until well mixed. Add the ice.
- Rinse the turkey, inside and out, under cold running water. Remove giblets and discard or save for another use. Some turkeys come with a gravy packet as well; remove it before roasting the bird.
- Add the turkey to the brine and refrigerate 8 to 12 hours, or overnight. Weight with a bag of ice to keep the bird submerged.
- Drain and pat dry with paper towels; discard the brine.
- To spatchcock the turkey: With a large knife or shears, cut the bird open along the backbone on both sides, through the ribs and remove the backbone.
- Once the bird is open, split the breastbone to spread the bird flat; this will allow it to roast evenly.
- Combine the melted butter and the remaining 1/4 cup of maple syrup and divide in half. Brush half of the mixture on the bird and sprinkle with Traeger Pork & Poultry Rub or salt and black pepper.
- Set aside the other half of the mixture until ready to use.
- When ready to cook, set the temperature to 350°F and preheat, lid closed for 15 minutes.
- Roast the turkey until the internal temperature in the thickest part of the breast reaches 165°F, about 2-3 hours.
- Brush with the remaining butter-maple syrup glaze the last 30 minutes of cooking.
- Let the turkey rest for 15 to 20 minutes before carving. Garnish, if desired, with fresh herbs and or kumquats. Enjoy!

6.15 Homemade Turkey Gravy
- **Ingredients:**
- 4 Cups Homemade Chicken Stock
- 2 Large Onions Cut Into 8th
- 4 Carrots, Rough Chop
- 4 Celery Stalks
- 8 Sprigs Thyme
- 8 Cloves Garlic, Peeled and Smashed
- 1 Turkey Neck
- 1 Cup Flour
- 1 Stick Butter, Cut into About 8 Pieces
- 1 Tsp Kosher Salt
- 1 Tsp Cracked Black Pepper

Instructions:

- When ready to cook, set the temperature to 350°F and preheat with the lid closed, for 15 minutes.
- In a large roasting pan, place turkey neck, onion, celery, carrot, garlic and thyme. Add 4 cups of chicken stock and sprinkle with salt and pepper.
- Place the prepped turkey on the rack into the roasting pan and place in the Traeger.
- Cook for 3-4 hours or until the breast reaches 160°F. Once taken off the grill, the turkey will continue to cook and will reach a finished internal temperature of 165°F.
- Strain the drippings into a saucepan and simmer on low.
- In a larger saucepan combine butter and flour with a whisk stirring until golden tan. This takes about 8 minutes, stirring constantly.
- Next whisk the drippings into the roux and cook until it comes to a boil. Season with salt and pepper and serve hot. Enjoy!

6.16 Roasted Honey Bourbon Glazed Turkey
Ingredients:

- Turkey
- 1 (16-18 Lbs.) Turkey
- 1/4 Cup Traeger Fin and Feather Rub
- Whiskey Glaze
- 1/2 Cup Bourbon
- 1/2 Cup Honey
- 1/4 Cup Brown Sugar
- 3 Tbsp Apple Cider Vinegar
- 1 Tbsp Dijon Mustard
- Salt and Pepper, To Taste

Instructions:

- When ready to cook, set the temperature to 375°F and preheat, lid closed for 15 minutes.
- Truss the turkey legs together. Season the exterior of the bird and the cavity with Traeger Fin and Feather Rub.
- Place the turkey directly on the grill grate and cook for 20-30 minutes at 375°F or until the skin begins to brown.
- After 30 minutes, reduce the temperature to 325°F and continue to cook until internal temperature registers 165°F when an instant read thermometer is inserted into the thickest part of the breast, about 3-4 hours.
- For the Whiskey Glaze: Combine all **Ingredients** in a small saucepan and bring to a boil. Reduce the temperature and let simmer 15-20 minutes or until thick enough to coat the back of a spoon. Remove from heat and set aside.
- During the last ten minutes of cooking, brush the glaze on the turkey while on the grill and cook until the glaze is set, about 10 minutes.
- Remove from grill and let rest 10-15 minutes before carving. Enjoy!

6.17 Roasted Autumn Brined Turkey Breast
Ingredients:

- 6 Cups Apple Cider
- 2 Cloves Garlic, Smashed
- 1/3 Cup Brown Sugar
- 1 Tbsp Allspice
- 1/3 Cup Kosher Salt
- 3 Bay Leaves
- 4 Cups Ice Water
- 1 Turkey Breast
- 1/2 Cup Plus Two Tbsp Unsalted Butter, Softened
- Traeger Pork and Poultry Rub

Instructions:

- For the Brine: In a large pot, combine 4 cups of the apple cider, the garlic cloves, brown sugar, allspice, salt, and bay leaves. Simmer on stove top for 5 minutes, stirring often.
- Take off stove top and add in the ice water.
- Place turkey in the brine and add water as needed until the turkey is fully submerged. Cover and refrigerate overnight.
- For the Cider Glaze: Boil the remaining 2 cups of apple cider in a saucepan until reduced to 1/4 cup, about 30-45 minutes. Whisk in butter and cool completely.
- After turkey has brined overnight, drain turkey and rinse.
- Using your fingers, take two tablespoons of the softened butter and smear it under the skin of the breast. Lightly season the turkey breast with Traeger Pork & Poultry Rub.
- When ready to cook, set the temperature to 325°F and preheat, lid closed for 15 minutes.
- Cook turkey until it reaches an internal temperature of 160°F, about 3-4 hrs. After the first 20 minutes of cooking, brush turkey with the cider glaze.
- If the breast starts to get too dark, cover it with foil. Let stand 30 minutes before carving. Enjoy!

6.18 Ultimate Smoked Turkey
Ingredients:

- 1 (18-20 Lb.) Turkey
- 1 Traeger Turkey Brine Kit
- 1/2 Cup Traeger Pork & Poultry Rub
- 1/2 Lb. Softened Butter

Instructions:

- The day before, brine the turkey according to the Traeger Turkey Brine Kit package directions.
- Remove from brine, rinse and pat dry. Season the inside cavity with Traeger Pork & Poultry Rub.
- Prepare the turkey by separating the skin from the breast creating a pocket to stuff the softened butter in. Cover the entire breast with 1/4-inch thickness of butter.
- Transfer to the fridge and let chill for at least 1 hour.
- Remove from the fridge and truss the legs and tuck the wing tips back around the bird.
- When ready to cook, set the Traeger to 225°F and preheat, lid closed for 15 minutes.
- Place the turkey in a roasting pan and place directly on the grill grate. Cook until the internal temperature reaches 100-110°F.
- Increase the temperature on the grill to 350°F and continue to cook until an instant read thermometer registers 160°F when inserted in the thickest part of the breast, about 3 to 4 hours total cook time. Turkey will continue to cook once taken off grill to reach a final temperature of 165°F in the breast.
- Remove the bird from the grill and let rest for at least 15 minutes before carving. Enjoy!

6.19 Smoked Wild Turkey Jerky
Ingredients:

- 3 Lb. Turkey Breast, Thinly Sliced
- 2 Cups Soy Sauce
- 1 Cup Brown Sugar
- 5 Garlic Cloves, Chopped
- 2 Tbsp Fresh Ginger, Chopped
- 1 Tbsp Ground Black Pepper
- 3 Tbsp Honey

Instructions:

- Combine all **Ingredients** in a large zip lock bag. Mix well. Place zip lock bag in a bowl and place in the refrigerator for 12 to 24 hours.
- When ready to cook, set temperature to 180°F and preheat, lid closed for 15 minutes.
- Drain the marinade and place the turkey strips on the grill.
- Let smoke for 4 hours or until the jerky is dry. Enjoy!

6.20 BBQ Chicken Breasts
Ingredients:

- 4-6 Boneless Skinless Chicken Breast
- 1 1/2 Cups Traeger Sweet & Heat BBQ Sauce
- Salt and Pepper, To Taste
- 1 Tbsp Chopped Parsley, To Garnish

Instructions:

- Place chicken breasts and 1 cup of Traeger Sweet & Heat BBQ sauce in a Ziploc bag and marinate overnight.
- Set temperature to High and preheat, lid closed for 15 minutes.
- Remove chicken from marinade and season with salt and pepper.
- Place directly on the grill grate and cook for 10 minutes on each side flipping once or until internal temperature reaches 150°F.
- Brush remaining sauce on chicken while on the grill and continue to cook 5-10 minutes longer or until a finished internal temperature of 165°F.
- Remove from grill and let rest 5 minutes before serving. Sprinkle with chopped parsley. Enjoy!

6.21 Beer-Brined Turkey
Ingredients:

- 1 (12-14 Lb.) Turkey
- 3 (12-Oz.) Cans or Bottles Dark Beer or Apple Cider
- 4 Qt. Cold Water
- 1-1/2 Cup Kosher Or 3/4 Cup Table Kosher Salt or Table Salt
- 1 Cup Dark Brown Sugar
- 3 Cloves Garlic, Smashed
- 1 Tbsp. Whole Black Peppercorns
- 1 Onion, Peeled and Cut into Quarters
- 4 Sprigs Each Fresh Rosemary, Thyme, Parsley, And Sage
- 3 Bay Leaves
- 2 Stalks Celery, Sliced Into 2" Pieces
- 1 Apple, Cut into Wedges
- Vegetable Oil, As Needed

Instructions:

- Thaw the turkey, if frozen, 3 days before you plan to eat the bird. Remove the giblets, if any.
- For the brine, in a large 5-gallon bucket or clean cooler, combine the beer, water, salt, and brown sugar and stir with a long-handled wooden spoon until the salt and sugar crystals are dissolved. Add the garlic and peppercorns.
- Add the turkey. Keep it submerged with a heavy pot lid or resealable bags of ice. Refrigerate for at least 8 hours.
- Remove the bird from the brine. Dry the turkey thoroughly, inside and out, with paper towels. Discard the brine.
- Put the onion, herbs, bay leaves, celery, and apple in the main cavity and tie the legs together with butcher's twine. Fold the wings behind the bird's back. Oil the outside of the bird.
- Put the turkey on a rack in a sturdy roasting pan. If you don't care to save the drippings, you can put the turkey directly on the grill grate.
- When ready to cook, set temperature to 350°F and preheat, lid closed for 15 minutes
- Put the roasting pan with the turkey on the grill grate and roast for 2-1/2 to 3 hours, or until a temperature probe inserted in the thickest part of the thigh reads 165°F.
- Let the turkey rest for 20 minutes before carving.
- *Cook times will vary depending on set and ambient

6.22 Cooking A Full Turkey on A Wood Pellet Grill & Smoker
Ingredients:

- 1 Eighteen Pound Turkey
- Dry Brine
- 6 tbsp Kosher Salt
- 2 tbsp Baking Soda
- Turkey Rub
- 1 cup Kosher Salt
- 1 cup Granulated Garlic
- 1 tbsp McCormick Poultry Seasoning

Instructions:

- Combine 6 tablespoons Morton's kosher salt with two tablespoons of baking powder in a bowl. Carefully pat your turkey dry with paper towels.
- Generously sprinkle it on all surfaces with the salt mixture by picking up the mixture between your thumb and fingers, holding it six to ten inches above the bird and letting the mixture shower down over the surface of the turkey for even coverage. The turkey should be well-coated with salt, though not completely encrusted. Leave in refrigerator for 24 hours.
- Prepare the smoker loading it up with either Apple or Cherry wood pellets but use whatever you think will work for you.
- Prepare an 8 to 18 lb. thawed or fresh turkey by removing the giblets and neck, draining the juices, and drying with paper towels. The turkey should be completely thawed for even, safe cooking. Do not stuff your turkey. Brush the skin with olive oil and insert an oven-safe meat thermometer deep into the lower thigh.
- Preheat the smoker to 275F degrees. Place the turkey breast side up on the grill. Place an oven thermometer alongside the turkey to monitor its temperature. I use a remote thermometer so you can monitor the temperature and also set an alarm when it hits 165 degrees (done).
- Try to plan for about 15-18 minutes per pound when you smoke at around 275F-300F degrees. If you like the skin to be crispy raise temperature to 300F.
- Check the temperature of your turkey after 3½ hours. Your turkey must pass through a critical range of 40F to 140F in 4 hours or less. If the internal temperature is low after 3½ hours, take your turkey off the smoker and finish it in the oven.
- When done, remove the turkey from the smoker, protecting your hands with BBQ Gloves, and let stand for 15 minutes before carving.

Chapter 7: Pork Recipes

7.1 Smoked Traeger Pulled Pork
Ingredients:

- 1 (6 To 9 Lb.) Whole Bone-In Pork Shoulder
- Traeger Big Game Rub
- 2 Cups Apple Cider

Instructions:

- When ready to cook, set the temperature to 250°F and preheat, lid closed for 15 minutes.
- While the Traeger comes to temperature, trim excess fat off pork butt. Generously season with Traeger Big Game Rub on all sides.
- Put pork butt fat side up directly on the grill grate and cook until the internal temperature reaches 160°F, about 3-5 hours. Remove the pork butt from the grill.
- On a large baking sheet, stack 4 large pieces of aluminum foil on top of each other, ensuring they are wide enough to wrap the pork butt entirely on all sides. If not, overlap the foil pieces to create a wider base.
- Place the pork butt in the center on the foil, then bring up the sides of the foil a little bit before pouring the apple cider on top of the pork butt. Wrap the foil tightly around the pork, ensuring the cider does not escape.
- Place the foil-wrapped pork butt back on the grill fat side up and cook until the internal temperature reaches 204°F, in the thickest part of the meat, about 3-4 hours longer depending on the size of the pork butt.
- Remove from the grill. Allow the pork to rest for 45 minutes in the foil packet. Remove the foil and pour off any excess liquid into a fat separator.
- Place the pork in a dish large enough to pull the meat, removing and discarding the bone and any excess fat. Add separated liquid back to pork and season to taste with additional Big Game Rub.
- Serve alone, in your favorite recipes, or on sandwiches. Refrigerate leftover pork in a covered container for up to 4 days. Enjoy!

7.2 Smoked Pig Shots Recipe
Ingredients:

- 1 Block Cream Cheese
- 2 Large Green Chile Peppers, diced (Substitute 1 Can Diced Green Chiles)
- 8 Oz Cheese, Shredded
- 1 Tbsp Chili Powder
- 2 Tbsp Meat Church Honey Hog
- 1 Package Thick Cut Bacon
- 1 Package of Your Favorite Smoked Sausage
- Toothpicks

Instructions:

- When ready to cook, start the Traeger grill on Smoke with the lid open until the fire is established (4 to 5 minutes). Set the temperature to 350 degrees F and preheat, lid closed, for 10 to 15 minutes.
- Allow the cream cheese to soften. Mix cream cheese, chiles, shredded cheese, chili powder and Honey Hog thoroughly in a mixing bowl. Set aside. Slice sausage into 1/2-inch slices.
- Cut bacon strips in half. Wrap bacon around the sausage, creating a bowl and secure with a toothpick.
- Fill the bowl with the cream cheese mixture. Top with more Honey Hog BBQ rub.
- Place the pig shots on the Traeger until the bacon is crispy and golden brown, about 45 to 60 minutes.
- Remove the pig shots from the grill and cool for 10 minutes, cream cheese will be hot. Enjoy!

7.3 Grilled German Sausage with A Smoky Traeger Twist
Ingredients:

- 4 Lbs. Ground Pork (80% Lean 20% Fat)
- 1 Lb. Ground Veal or Ground Beef
- 2 Tbsp Jacobsen Salt
- 1 Tsp Instacart Or Morton's Tender quick Curing Salt
- 1 Tbsp Ground Nutmeg
- 2 Tsp Ground Mace
- 1 Tsp Ground Ginger
- 1 Cup Cold Milk
- 2 Eggs
- 1 Cup Non-Fat Dry Milk Powder

Instructions:

- Combine salt, tender quick, nutmeg, mace and ginger in a large pitcher or small bowl.
- Add the milk and eggs and beat until well combined. Pour the egg mixture over the ground meat and mix gently.
- Using your hands, mix in the milk powder until evenly distributed.
- Form the meat into sausage links.
- When ready to cook, set the temperature to 450°F and preheat, lid closed for 15 minutes.
- Smoke for approximately 2 hours or until the internal temperature reaches 175 degrees F.
- Serve immediately or refrigerate until ready to serve. Enjoy!

7.4 Texas Style Smoked Pulled Pork
Ingredients:

- 1/2 cup kosher salt USE KOSHER, NOT TABLE SALT
- 1/2 cup ground black pepper
- 1/3 cup paprika
- 1/2 cup brown sugar
- 2 tbsp granulated garlic
- 2 tbsp granulated onion
- 2 tbsp cayenne pepper
- 1 tbsp celery salt
- PULLED PORK
- 8-10 lb. pork shoulder butt
- 2 tbsp yellow mustard
- 1 cup apple cider vinegar/apple juice in a spritzer bottle

Instructions:

- Prepare your pork butt. trimming any excess fat leaving about 1/4 inch of fat on the fat cap side. Trim off any unwanted glands or cartridge as well. Pat dry with a paper towel, then spread a light coat of mustard.
- With your rub ingredients combined, liberally coat your pork butt. You shouldn't see anything but your rub on the pork.
- Preheat your smoker to 235. Place your pork butt, fat side up on the grates. Close the smoker and don't peek for about 2 hours. Spritz every hour after the 2-hour mark.
- At around the 4-5-hour mark start probing for temperature. When you get to about 160, it's time to wrap. Taking a couple 18×30 sheets of aluminum foil. Remove your pork butt from the grates with a towel and place on the foil fat side down; spritz one more time. Wrap as tightly as possible so that you don't lose any of that bark. Double wrap so that the foil doesn't tear on the grates.
- At this point your pork butt has taken all the smoke it's going to get. You can either leave the temperature at 235, or increase to around 275 to speed up the process. Place the pork butt fat side down onto the grate and close. Probe for tenderness and temperature at the 7- or 8-hour mark until the internal temperature is around 200-205. If you can easily pull the blade from the meat, you're ready to take off the grill.
- Keep wrapped and let rest of the grill for about 30-45 minutes. Pull away and enjoy!

7.5 Spice Rubbed Pork Tenderloin
Ingredients:

- 2 pork tenderloins
- 2 tsp dried oregano
- 1 tsp cumin
- 1 tsp chili powder
- 1 tsp paprika
- 4 garlic cloves, minced or pushed through a press
- ½ C lime juice
- ¾ C fresh orange juice
- 2 tsp orange rind, finely grated
- ¼ C olive oil
- ¼ C fresh mint leaves, minced
- ¼ C fresh cilantro leaves, minced
- ½ tsp salt
- Grinding of fresh pepper

Instructions:

- In a small bowl, mix oregano, cumin, chili powder and paprika together. Divide into two equal portions. Set one portion aside for later use.
- Pat tenderloins dry with paper towel and coat the meat with half of the rub. Gently massage it into the surface of the meat then place the tenderloins into a food safe, re-sealable plastic bag.
- In a small bowl combine the orange juice, orange rind, lime juice, olive oil, mint, cilantro and garlic. Pour this marinade mixture over the tenderloins and seal the bag. Refrigerate for at least 4 hours or overnight, turning the bag occasionally.
- Preheat the Memphis Wood Pellet Grill to 375 degrees F.
- Remove tenderloins from the bag and pat dry. Add salt and pepper to the reserved portion of spice mixture. Sprinkle over the tenderloin and rub gently into the surface of the meat.
- Place seasoned pork tenderloin on the lower rack of the pre-heated Memphis Pellet Grill. Close the lid and cook until the internal temperature of the meat reaches 145 degrees F (about 35 minutes).
- Remove from grill and rest for 5-10 minutes before serving.

7.6 Apple Cider Braised Smoked BBQ Pulled Pork
Ingredients:

- 7–9 lb. bone-in pork butt/shoulder roast
- RUB
- 4 tablespoons brown sugar
- 1 tablespoon garlic powder
- 1 tablespoon onion powder
- 1 tablespoon kosher salt
- 1/2 tablespoon pepper
- 1.5 tablespoons smoked paprika
- 2 teaspoons dry mustard
- 1 tablespoon coriander
- 1 tablespoon chili powder
- SPRAY
- 1/2 cup apple cider
- 1/2 cup apple cider vinegar
- BRAISING
- 2 cups apple cider
- 3–4 sweet, crisp red apples, peeled and sliced
- 2 onions, sliced
- SAUCE
- 1 cup ketchup
- 1/2 cup apple jelly
- 1/4 cup apple cider
- 1 tablespoon apple cider vinegar

- 1 teaspoon liquid smoke
- 1/2 tablespoon Worcestershire sauce
- 1 teaspoon chili powder
- 1/2 teaspoon onion powder
- 1 cup pan juices from roast (fat separated)

Instructions:

- Pat roast dry. Combine all rub ingredients and pat on all sides of roast, rubbing in well. Cover roast and let sit overnight in the fridge.
- When ready to cook, preheat smoker to 225 degrees and smoke roast directly on grill for 5 hours. While cooking, combine spray ingredients in a clean spray bottle and spritz roast all over once every hour.
- While roast is smoking, combine all sauce ingredients and whisk together in a pan. Set aside until pan juices are ready.
- After smoking, transfer your roast to either your slow cooker (if it will fit, remember you have more stuff going in there!) or a roasting pan, or disposable roasting pan (if you'll continue cooking on the smoker.)
- Place apples, onions, and 2 cups apple cider around the roast in the roasting pan. Cover with lid, or tightly with foil. Cook in slow cooker on high for 6-7 hours (or low for more like 8-10 if you want/need to drag it out, overnight for example.) If you are cooking in the oven, set temperature to 275 degrees. In the smoker, you can increase temperature to 275 as well. Cook until internal temperature reaches 200-210 degrees, usually about 6-7 hours.
- Let pork rest, covered for at least 15 minutes (longer is just fine) before discarding bones, separating fat, etc.
- Pour pan juices into a fat separator. Pour 1 cup of juices into your BBQ sauce and bring to a simmer. Simmer for about 15 minutes until slightly thickened.
- Pour a little of the remaining juices over shredded pork. Use a slotted spoon to grab the onions and apples and mix them in with the pork. Serve alone or on rolls or over rice. Freezes great! Excellent on nachos, pizzas, and more.

7.7 Bourbon Brown Sugar Smoked Pork Loin
Ingredients:

For the pork:

- 1 center-cut piece of pork loin (2½ to 3 pounds)
- 3 tablespoons Tennessee whiskey
- 2 tablespoons of your favorite barbecue rub
- 3 tablespoons Dijon mustard
- ½ cup firmly packed brown sugar
- 4 slices bacon

For the glaze:

- 3 tablespoons salted butter
- 3 tablespoons brown sugar
- 3 tablespoons Dijon mustard
- 3 tablespoons Tennessee whiskey
- Barbecue sauce (optional), for serving

Instructions:

- Butterfly the pork loin: Using a very sharp knife, cut the roast almost in half lengthwise through one side (stop about 1 inch from the opposite side). Open the roast up as you would a book. Sprinkle the inside of the roast with 1 tablespoon of the whiskey and let it marinate for 5 minutes. Sprinkle a third of the rub over the inside of the roast. Spread the mustard on top with a spatula, then sprinkle the brown sugar on top of the mustard. Sprinkle the remaining 2 tablespoons of whiskey on top of the brown sugar. Fold the roast back together (like closing a book) and sprinkle the remaining rub over the outside.
- Cut four 12-inch pieces of butcher's string. Position the pieces of string on the work surface so that they are parallel and roughly 2 inches apart. Place a slice of bacon across the strings so that it is perpendicular to and in the center of them. Set the roast on top of the bacon, positioning its long side parallel to the bacon. Place a slice of bacon on top of the roast. Press the remaining 2 slices against the long sides of the roast. Tie each piece of string together around the roast so that they hold the slices of bacon against it. Set the pork roast aside.
- Make the glaze: Combine the butter, brown sugar, mustard, and whiskey in a saucepan and boil until syrupy, 4 to 6 minutes. Set the glaze aside.
- Set up the grill for indirect grilling and preheat to medium. If using a gas grill, place all of the wood chips or chunks in the smoker box or in a smoker pouch and run the grill on high until you see smoke, then reduce the heat to medium. If using a

charcoal grill, place a large drip pan in the center, preheat the grill to medium, then toss all of the wood chips or chunks on the coals.

- When ready to cook, place the pork roast on the hot grate, over the drip pan and away from the heat and cover the grill. Cook the roast until cooked through, 1 to 1½ hours. To test for doneness, insert an instant-read meat thermometer into the side of the roast: The internal temperature should be about 160°F. Start basting the roast with some of the glaze after 30 minutes and continue basting every 15 minutes. If you are using a charcoal grill and the pork is not done after 1 hour, you'll need to add 12 fresh coals to each side.
- Transfer the cooked roast to a cutting board and let it rest for 5 minutes, then remove and discard the strings. Slice the roast crosswise and drizzle any remaining glaze over it. If you like, serve barbecue sauce alongside.

Chapter 8: Seafood Recipes

8.1 Spicy Shrimp Skewers
Ingredients:

- 2 Lbs. Shrimp, Peeled, And Deveined
- 6 Oz Thai Chilies
- 6 Cloves Garlic
- 2 Tbsp Winemakers Blend Napa Valley Rub
- 1-1/2 Tsp Sugar
- 1-1/2 Tbsp White Vinegar
- 3 Tbsp Olive Oil
- Bamboo or Metal Skewers

Instructions:

- Place all ingredients besides shrimp in a blender and blend until a course textured paste is reached.
- Place shrimp in a bowl, add chili garlic mixture and place in fridge to marinate for at least 30 minutes.
- Remove from fridge and thread shrimp onto bamboo or metal skewers.
- When ready to cook, start the Traeger according to grill instructions. Set the temperature to 450 degrees F (set to 500 degrees F if using a WiFIRE enables grill) and preheat, lid closed, for 10 to 15 minutes.
- Place shrimp on grill and cook for 2 to 3 minutes per side or until shrimp are pink and firm to touch. Enjoy!

8.2 Baja-Style Fish Tacos
Ingredients:

- 1 Lb. White Fish Such as Cod, Monkfish, Or Halibut (Skinless)
- 2 Limes
- 2 Tsp. Dijon-Style Mustard
- 1/2 Tsp. Salt
- 1/2 Tsp. Black Pepper, Freshly Ground
- 1/2 Cup Vegetable Oil, Or Olive Oil
- 2 Cloves Garlic, Minced
- As Needed Traeger Cajun Rub
- 8 Corn Tortillas
- For Serving Shredded Cabbage, Diced Red Onions, Cilantro Leaves, Pickled Jalapeno Slices, Diced Avocado, Pico De Gallo Or Salsa, Sour Cream

Instructions:

- Juice one lime. Cut the other lime in wedges; set aside until serving time.
- Make the marinade: In a small mixing bowl, combine the lime juice, mustard, and salt and pepper. Slowly whisk in the oil, then stir in the garlic.
- Place the fish in a resealable plastic bag, pour the marinade over it, and refrigerate for no more than 1 hour.
- When ready to cook, start the Traeger grill on Smoke with the lid open until the fire is established (4 to 5 minutes). Set the temperature to 400F (High on a 3-position controller) and preheat, lid closed, for 10 to 15 minutes.
- Remove the fish from the marinade and pat off any excess marinade with paper towels. Season generously on both sides with Traeger Cajun Rub.
- Arrange the fish on the grill grate and grill until the fish is opaque and flakes easily when pressed with a fork. (There is no need to turn it.) Remove to a cutting board and cut into bite-size chunks. Meanwhile, warm the tortillas on the Traeger until pliant and hot.
- Arrange the fish, tortillas, and suggested accompaniments on a large platter. Garnish with the reserved lime wedges. Serve immediately.

8.3 Traeger Jerk Shrimp
Ingredients:

- 1 Tbsp Brown Sugar
- 1 Tbsp Smoked Paprika
- 1 Tsp Garlic Powder
- 1/4 Tsp Ground Thyme
- 1/4 Tsp Ground Cayenne
- 1/8 Tsp Smoked Paprika
- 1 Tsp Sea Salt
- Zest Of 1 Lime
- 3 Tbsp Olive Oil
- 2 Lbs. Shrimp, Peel On

Instructions:

- Combine spices, salt, and lime zest in a small bowl and mix. Place shrimp into a large bowl, then drizzle in the olive oil, Add the spice mixture and toss to combine, making sure every shrimp is kissed with deliciousness.
- When ready to cook, set the temperature to 450°F and preheat, lid closed for 15 minutes
- Arrange the shrimp on the grill and cook for 2 – 3 minutes per side, until firm, opaque, and cooked through.
- Serve with lime wedges, fresh cilantro, mint, and Caribbean Hot Pepper Sauce. Enjoy!

8.4 Traeger Smoked Mussels
Ingredients:

- Mussels
- 1/4 Cup Butter
- 1 Tbsp Smoked Paprika
- 4 Garlic Cloves, Minced
- 1 Cup Apple Cider
- 3 Lbs. Mussels, Cleaned & Scrubbed
- Fresh Lemons & Crusty Bread to Serve
- Salsa Verde
- 1 Small Bunch Fresh Chives
- 1 Small Bunch Tarragon
- 1 Small Bunch Basil
- 1 Small Bunch Flat-Leaf Parsley
- 1 Garlic Clove, Peeled and Roughly Chopped
- Juice Of 1/2 Lemon
- 200 MLX Extra-Virgin Olive Oil
- Sea Salt & Fresh Crackled Black Pepper

Instructions:

- When ready to cook, set the temperature to 350°F and preheat, lid closed for 15 minutes
- Heat a cast-iron (or oven-safe) pan over medium heat, and melt the butter. When melted, add the garlic and cook for 30 seconds (keep watch that it doesn't burn), then pour in the apple cider and bring to a simmer. Add the mussels, cover with a tight-fitting lid, and transfer to the Traeger. Cook for 8 – 10 minutes, or until the mussels have opened (discard any mussels that do not open).
- While the mussels are cooking, crack on with the salsa Verde. Combine the fresh herbs and garlic in a food processor (or high-powered blender) and finely chop. Add the lemon juice and season with salt and pepper. With the blender running on low, drizzle in the olive oil in a slow & steady stream until thick and glorious.
- Serve up those beautiful wood-fire kissed mussels with the salsa Verde, lemon wedges, and crusty bread. Enjoy!

8.5 Grilled Lobster Tails
Ingredients:

- 2 Lobster Tails, 8-10 Oz Each
- 8 Tbsp Butter
- 2 Tbsp Lemon Juice
- 1 Tsp Paprika
- 1/4 Tsp Garlic Salt
- 1/4 Tsp Old Bay Seasoning
- 1/4 Tsp Freshly Ground Black Pepper
- 2 Tbsp Fresh Parsley, Chopped

Instructions:

- Prepare the lobster by cutting down the middle of the tough shell toward the tail with kitchen shears. Using your fingers, gently pry the meat from the shell, keeping it attached at the base of the tail. Lift the meat so it is resting on top of the split shell (again, keeping it attached at the base of the tail).
- Make a slit down the middle of the meat to butterfly it open on top. Place the lobster tails on a rimmed baking sheet.
- Melt the butter in a small saucepan over medium-low heat. Whisk in the lemon juice, paprika, garlic salt, Old Bay Seasoning, pepper, and parsley.
- Pour about 1 tablespoon of the butter mixture over each lobster tail. Keep the remaining butter mixture warm.
- When ready to cook, set temperature to High and preheat, lid closed for 15 minutes.
- Remove the lobster tails from the baking sheet and arrange them directly on the grill grate. Cook for 25 to 30 minutes, or until the meat is white and opaque.
- Transfer lobster tails to a platter and serve with the reserved butter mixture. Enjoy!

8.6 Garlic Salmon
Ingredients:

- 1 2-3 Lb. Salmon Filet, Skin On
- 1/4 Cup Olive Oil
- 2 Tbsp Garlic, Minced
- 1/2 Tbsp Parsley, Minced
- Traeger Fin & Feather Rub
- Lemon Wedges, For Serving

Instructions:

- Line a baking sheet with butcher paper or parchment. Place the salmon skin side down on the baking sheet and season the filet with the Traeger Fin & Feather Rub. In a small bowl combine olive oil, garlic, and parsley. Set aside.
- When ready to cook, set temperature to High and preheat, lid closed for 15 minutes.
- Brush the salmon with the garlic mixture and transfer the baking sheet to the grill. Cook until the internal temperature reaches 140°F (about 20-25 minutes), or until the fish flakes easily.
- Remove from the grill and brush with any extra garlic mixture you may have and serve with lemon wedges. Enjoy!

8.7 Grilled Penang Curry Salmon
Ingredients:

- Penang Curry Salmon
- 1 (12 Oz) Jar Thai fusions Penang Curry
- 1 (4-7 Lb.) Salmon Fillet
- 2 Sprigs Thai Basil, Roughly Chopped
- 1/2 Red Bell Pepper Sliced Thinly, Lengthwise
- 1 Lime, Sliced into Thin Crosscut Pieces
- Mussels with Prawns (Optional)
- 1/2 Lb. Prawns, Shelled and Deveined
- 1/2 Lb. Mussels Debearded And Washed
- Handful Thai Basil, Chopped

Instructions:

- Season both sides of the salmon with salt and pepper.
- Brush a little canola oil on the salmon fillet and marinate with a 1/2 cup of Thai fusions Penang Curry in a shallow pan. Cover and marinate at room temperature for about 30 minutes.
- When ready to cook, set temperature to High and preheat, lid closed for 15 minutes.
- Brush some canola oil onto the grill so the salmon won't stick. Place salmon fillet directly on the grill grate and brush on about another 1/4 cup of Thai fusions Penang Curry and top with sliced red bell pepper and lime slices.
- Grill salmon until an internal temperature of 145°F, about 10-15 minutes.
- For the Mussels and Prawns: Pour last 1/4 cup of Penang Curry into a sauce pan, add prawns, mussels, Thai basil and cover sauce pan and finish on the Traeger. When the mussels have opened, take off the grill and set aside.
- Take salmon off the grill as gently as possible and top salmon with mussels and prawns if desired. Garnish with Thai basil. Enjoy!

8.8 Seared Lemon Garlic Scallops
Ingredients:

- Scallops
- 1 Dozen U-20 Scallops
- Kosher Salt
- 1 Tbsp Butter
- 1 Tbsp Olive Oil
- Chopped Parsley, To Garnish
- Lemon Zest, To Garnish
- Garlic Butter
- 4 Tbsp Butter, Melted
- Juice Of 1 Lemon
- 1 Clove Garlic, Minced

Instructions:

- When ready to cook, set the temperature to 400°F and preheat, lid closed for 15 minutes.
- Remove the frill if it is still intact. Pat the scallops dry with a paper towel. Season liberally with salt and a bit of black pepper.
- When the grill is hot, place the butter and olive oil on the skillet. When the butter has melted, place the scallops on the skillet. Close the lid and cook for about 2 minutes until seared and browned on one side.
- While the scallops cook, combine the melted butter and garlic in a small bowl.
- Flip the scallops, spoon a couple tablespoons of garlic butter over the top and cook for 1 minute longer.
- Remove from the grill, add a little more garlic butter if desired and finish with parsley and lemon zest. Enjoy!

8.9 Whole Grilled Red Snapper
Ingredients:

- Red Snapper
- 1 Whole Red Snapper, Rinse and Pat Dry
- 2 Tbsp Olive Oil
- 1/2 Tbsp Kosher Salt
- 1 Tsp Black Pepper
- 1/4 Cup Butter, Melted
- 1/4 Cup Harissa
- Salad
- 1 Bunch Watercress, Trimmed and Washed
- 2 Cherry Peppers, Thinly Sliced
- 3 Scallions, Thinly Sliced
- 2 Tbsp Chopped Cilantro
- 2 Tbsp Mint Leaves Torn
- 2 Limes, Juiced
- 1 Tsp Brown Sugar
- 1/4 Tsp Fish Sauce
- 1/4 Cup Olive Oil
- Salt and Pepper, To Taste

Instructions:

- In a medium bowl combine melted butter and harissa.
- When ready to cook, set the temperature to High and preheat, lid closed for 15 minutes.
- Coat the exterior of the fish with olive oil and season with salt and pepper on both sides. Place fish directly on the grill grate, brush with the harissa-butter mixture and cook for 15-20 minutes.
- While the fish cooks, prepare the salad. In a small bowl combine the lime juice, brown sugar, fish sauce, salt and pepper. While whisking, slowly stream in olive oil. In a medium bowl combine the watercress, peppers, scallions, cilantro and mint. Wait to dress the salad until ready to serve.
- Flip the fish and brush the other side with harissa-butter mixture. Close the lid and continue to cook 10-15 minutes more until the internal temperature registers 145°F.

- Carefully remove the fish from the grill and place on a serving platter. Drizzle the dressing over the greens, season to taste with salt and pepper and mix to coat.
- Pile the salad over the top of the fish and drizzle the fish with remaining dressing if desired. Enjoy!

8.10 Roasted Halibut in Parchment
Ingredients:

- 4 Ea. (4 Oz) Fish Fillets, Such as Salmon, Halibut or Snapper, Pin Bones Removed
- Extra-Virgin Olive Oil
- Kosher Salt and Freshly Ground Pepper
- 2 Lemons, Preferably Meyer, Ends Trimmed, Cut Into 12 Slices
- Kernels From 2 Ears of Corn
- 16 Asparagus Spears, Bottoms Trimmed, Sliced Into 1/2-Inch Pieces
- 2 Tbsp Finely Chopped Assorted Herbs, Such as Basil, Chives, Or Parsley
- Equipment: 4 Pieces Parchment Paper

Instructions:

- When ready to cook, set the temperature to High and preheat, lid closed for 15 minutes.
- Cut four pieces of parchment paper or Traeger butcher paper each 18" long.
- Place a fish fillet on the center of a piece of parchment. Season with a pinch each of salt and pepper, then drizzle with olive oil. Place three lemon slices on the fillet, overlapping them slightly to cover the fish.
- Sprinkle one-fourth each of the corn, asparagus, and tomatoes (if using) evenly around the fish, then drizzle with a little olive oil and season again with a small pinch each of salt and pepper.
- Bring the long sides of the paper together, and fold the top edges down together to create a 1-inch seal, then continue to fold down tightly over the fish and vegetables.
- Twist the open ends of the parchment in opposite directions to prevent steam from escaping.
- Repeat the process with the remaining ingredients and parchment and place the packets on a baking sheet. If not cooking immediately, refrigerate for up to 4 hours.
- Place the baking sheet on the Traeger and bake until the packets are lightly browned and have puffed up, about 15 minutes.
- Transfer each packet to a plate and let stand for 5 minutes. Using sharp scissors, cut an X into the center of each packet and carefully pull back the parchment and sprinkle with the herbs.
- Serve immediately. Enjoy!

8.11 Grilled Lobster with Lemon Garlic Butter Recipe
Ingredients:

- Grilled Lobster
- (4) 1 1/2 Lb. Live Lobsters
- 2 Tbsp 2 T Olive Oil
- 2 Lemons, Sliced
- Flat Leaf Parsley, To Serve
- Lemon Garlic Butter
- 3/4 Cup Butter, Softened
- 2 Tbsp Flat Leaf Parsley, Finely Diced
- 1 Tbsp Minced Shallot
- 2 Cloves Garlic, Minced
- 1 Tbsp Lemon Juice
- 1 Tbsp Lemon Zest
- 1/2 Tsp Sea Salt
- 1/2 Tsp Fresh Cracked Black Pepper

Instructions:

- Bring a large stockpot of water to a rapid boil. Working in batches as necessary, submerge the lobster in the water head first, then cover with a lid. Cook for 5 minutes, then transfer to an ice-bath to cool and stop the cooking process.
- In a small saucepan, melt the butter over medium low heat. When melted, add the remaining ingredients and whisk together until smooth. Set aside.
- Using a very sharp knife, split the lobster into 2 halves. Clean out the tomalley from the body and discard. Brush the lobster halves all over with olive oil.
- When ready to cook, set temperature to High and preheat, lid closed for 15 minutes.
- When hot, place the lobsters on the grill, flesh side down, and cook for 4 minutes. Turn, and spoon about 2 tsp of compound butter onto each lobster half. As the butter begins to melt, baste with a brush all over the flesh. Cook for 4-5 minutes until cooked through and coated in melted butter.
- Serve immediately with sliced lemons and parsley. Enjoy!

8.12 BBQ Oysters
Ingredients:

- BBQ Oysters
- 12 Oysters, Shucked
- 1 Bunch Green Onions, Chopped
- 8 Oz Shredded Pepper Jack Cheese
- 1/4 Cup Seasoned Bread Crumbs
- Traeger Sweet & Heat BBQ Sauce
- Compound Butter
- 1 Lb. Butter, Unsalted
- 1 Tbsp Meat Church the Gospel or Honey Hog BBQ Rub
- 1/2 Bunch Green Onions, Minced
- 2 Cloves Garlic, Minced

Instructions:

- When ready to cook, start the Traeger according to grill instructions. Set the temperature to 375 degrees F and preheat, lid closed, for 10 to 15 minutes.
- For the compound butter: Allow the butter to soften. Combine butter, garlic, onion and BBQ Rub thoroughly.
- Lay the butter on parchment paper or plastic wrap. Roll it up to form a log and tie each end with butcher's twine. Place in the freezer for an hour to solidify. You can use this butter on any grilled meats to enhance the flavor. You can also use a high-quality butter to replace the compound butter.
- Shuck the oysters keeping all of the juice in the shell.
- Sprinkle the oysters with bread crumbs and place directly on the Traeger. Cook them for 5 minutes. You will be looking for the edge of the oyster to start to curl slightly.
- After 5 minutes place a spoonful of butter in the oysters. After the butter melts, add a pinch of pepper jack cheese.
- Remove the oysters after 6 minutes on the grill total. Top oysters with a squirt of BBQ sauce and a few chopped onions. Allow to cool for 5 minutes, then enjoy!

8.13 Maple Glazed Salmon
Ingredients:

- 1/2 C + 3 Tbsp soy sauce
- 1 C maple syrup (the real stuff)
- Really fresh thick salmon, skin on (I prefer Sockeye, however, that is the strongest of the selection. If you're working with some people you hope to convert, the farm-raised stuff is a little lighter.)

Instructions:

- Mix a 1/2 C of soy with a 1/2 C of maple syrup in a dish big enough that the salmon fits flat but not so deep that the skin is covered.
- Put in the fridge. This isn't a "longer is better" type of meat to marinate, so 15 minutes per inch should suffice with at least 30 minutes total, regardless of size. (For 2 inches, 45-60 minutes is a safe window.)
- Set grill to 400 degrees F and lightly oil just enough of the grate to accommodate the fish flesh side down.

- Heat 1/2 C of maple syrup and 3 Tbsp of soy sauce in a skillet pan (not cast iron and not non-stick) until the glaze thickens a bit. Note: You can also have some fun here. Brown sugar, honey, mustard and cherry juice can all be mixed around for good flavors. Even adding some spice to the party can change this dish around.
- Brush the salmon with the glaze and put it flesh side down on the hot grill and shut the lid.
- Flip fish after a few minutes. If it is ready to be turned over (and you've oiled your grill grates), it shouldn't stick.
- Cook the salmon until the internal temperature reaches 140 degrees F. Less is fine, more is okay, but understand that a little rare for fresh salmon will never hurt you, but a little too much will destroy the meal.

8.14 Lemon Garlic Smoked Salmon Recipe
Ingredients:

- 6 5 oz Prime Waters Seafood Salmon Filets
- 4 tbsp softened butter
- 2 tsp lemon juice
- 1 tsp lemon zest
- 1 tsp salt
- 1 tsp pepper
- 1 clove garlic minced

Instructions:

- Preheat wood pellet smoker to 350 degrees F
- Combine all of the ingredients (except the salmon) in a bowl and mix well.
- Add a generous amount of the butter mixture on top of each filet of salmon, and top with lemon slices if desired
- Add each filet to the wood pellet grill and cook until an internal temperature of 125 degrees is reached.
- Remove the filets from the grill and tent with aluminum foil. Let rest for 10 minutes before serving.
- Garnish with lemon slices and additional spices for presentation

8.15 Easy and Flavorful Smoked Tilapia
Ingredients:

- 6 tilapia fillets
- 3 tbsp./45 ml vegetable oil
- 2 tbsp./30 ml fresh lemon juice
- 1/2 tsp./2.5 ml garlic powder
- 1 tsp./5 ml kosher salt
- 1/2 tsp./2.5 ml lemon pepper

Instructions:

- Prepare smoker for a 2-hour smoke.
- Wash fish and remove all bones. Combine oil, lemon juice, garlic powder, salt, and lemon pepper in a small bowl. Brush liquid mixture onto both sides of the tilapia fillets.
- Place in the smoker for 1 1/2 to 2 hours.
- When finished, remove from heat and serve.

Chapter 9: Desserts Recipes

9.1 Strawberry Shortbread
Ingredients:

- 1 Qt. Strawberries, Washed, Stemmed, And Sliced
- To Taste, About 1 To 2 Tbsp. Sugar, For Strawberries
- 1 To 2 Tsp. Grand Marnier Or Triple Sec (Optional)
- 2 Cups, Plus More for Flouring Board All-Purpose Flour
- 2 To 3 Tbsp. Sugar
- 1 Tbsp. Baking Powder
- 1/4 Tsp. Salt
- 1/4 Tsp. Cinnamon
- 2 Tbsp. Butter, Cold, Cubed
- 2 Tbsp. Shortening, Cold
- 2/3 Cup Milk or Half and Half
- As Needed Butter, Melted
- For Serving Sweetened Whipped Cream

Instructions:

- In a mixing bowl, combine the strawberries and sugar to taste (1 to 2 tablespoons are usually enough to sweeten the berries). Add the Grand Marnier, if using, and stir, crushing some of the berries slightly to release their juices. Cover and refrigerate until serving time.
- Sift the 2 cups of flour, sugar, baking powder, salt, and cinnamon into a mixing bowl. (Or just put the ingredients into the bowl and whisk to combine.) Cut the butter and shortening into the dry ingredients with a pastry blender, fork, or knife until the mixture is reduced to pea-size clumps. Make a well in the center, and pour in the milk. Stir until just combined. Do not overmix.
- Lightly flour a cutting board or countertop and dump the shortcake mixture onto it. Knead lightly to bring the dough together. Pat into a 1/2-inch thick circle and cut rounds out with a biscuit cutter or an upended glass. Transfer to an ungreased baking sheet. Brush the tops of the shortcakes with the melted butter.
- When ready to cook, start the Traeger grill on Smoke with the lid open until the fire is established (4 to 5 minutes). Set the temperature to 425F or High and preheat, lid closed, for 10 to 15 minutes.
- Put the pan with the shortcakes on the grill grate and close the lid. Bake for 10 minutes, or until the shortcakes have risen and are nicely browned. Let cool slightly, then slit in half with a knife. Divide the strawberries between the bottom halves of the shortcakes, then replace the tops. Top with sweetened whipped cream.

9.2 Leave No Trace Chocolate-Chunk Oatmeal Cookies
Ingredients:

- 1 Cup Old-Fashioned Rolled Oats (Not Instant or Quick-Cooking)
- 1 Cup All-Purpose Flour
- 1/2 Tsp. Baking Powder
- 1/2 Tsp. Baking Soda
- 1/4 Tsp. Salt
- 1/2 Cup (1 Stick) Butter, Softened
- 1/2 Cup Peanut Butter (Smooth or Chunky)
- 1/2 Cup Sugar
- 1/2 Cup Brown Sugar, Firmly Packed
- 1 Large Egg
- 1 1/2 Tsp. Vanilla
- 1 Generous Cup Semi-Sweet Chocolate Chunks or Chips, Coarsely Chopped

Instructions:

- When ready to cook, set temperature to 225°F and preheat, lid closed for 15 minutes.
- Line a sturdy rimmed baking sheet with parchment paper.
- Spread the oats in an even layer on the baking sheet. Place the baking sheet on the grill grate and smoke the oats, stirring once. Remove from the grill. Increase the temperature of the Traeger to 375°F

- In the meantime, make the cookie dough: Let the smoked oats cool completely. Lift the sides of the parchment paper up and tip the oats into a mixing bowl. (Return the parchment paper to the baking sheet; you'll reuse it for the cookies.) Add the flour, baking powder, baking soda, and salt and stir to combine. Set aside.
- In another bowl - such as the bowl of a stand mixer - combine the butter, peanut butter, and sugar.
- Mix on medium-high speed (you can use a hand-held mixer or a wooden spoon and elbow grease) until the mixture is light and fluffy.
- Beat in the egg and vanilla. Gradually add the oatmeal-flour mixture using low speed. Stir in the chocolate chunks by hand.
- Drop the dough by heaping tablespoons onto the prepared baking sheet and flatten slightly with the back of a tablespoon.
- Bake for about 12 minutes, or until the cookies have spread and are lightly browned. Remove the baking sheet from the grill. Let the cookies firm up for a minute or two, then transfer to a wire cooling rack to cool.
- Repeat with the remainder of the dough. Store in an airtight container. Enjoy!

9.3 Double Chocolate Chip Brownie Pie
Ingredients:

- 1 Cup Butter
- 1 Cup Brown Sugar
- 1 Cup Sugar
- 2 Tsp. Vanilla
- 4 Eggs
- 2 Cups All-Purpose Flour
- 2/3 Cup Cocoa Powder
- 1 Tsp. Baking Soda
- 1 Tsp. Salt
- 1 1/2 Cup Semi-Sweet Chocolate Chips, Divided
- 3/4 Cup White Chocolate Chips
- 3/4 Cup Nuts (Optional)
- 1, 8-Oz. Hot Fudge Sauce
- 1-2 Tbsp. Guinness

Instructions:

- Coat the inside of a 10-inch pie plate with non-stick cooking spray.
- When ready to cook, set the temperature to 350°F and preheat, lid closed for 15 minutes.
- Melt 1/2 cup of the semi-sweet chocolate chips in the microwave. Cream together butter, brown sugar and granulated sugar. Beat in the eggs, adding one at a time and mixing after each egg, and the vanilla. Add in the melted chocolate chips.
- On a large piece of wax paper, sift together the cocoa powder, flour, baking soda and salt. Lift up the corners of the paper and pour slowly into the butter mixture.
- Beat until the dry ingredients are just incorporated. Stir in the remaining semi-sweet chocolate chips, white chocolate chips, and the nuts. Press the dough into the prepared pie pan.
- Place the brownie pie on the grill and bake for 45-50 minutes or until the pie is set in the middle. Rotate the pan halfway through cooking. If the top or edges begin to brown, cover the top with a piece of aluminum foil.
- In a microwave-safe measuring cup, heat the fudge sauce in the microwave. Stir in the Guinness.
- Once the brownie pie is done, allow to sit for 20 minutes. Slice into wedges and top with the fudge sauce. Enjoy

10.1 Baked Wood-Fired Pizza
Ingredients:

- Dough
- 2/3 Cup Warm Water (Between 100-110°F)
- 2 1/2 Tsp Active Dry Yeast
- 1/2 Tsp Granulated Sugar
- 1 Tsp Kosher Salt
- 1 Tbsp Oil
- 1 3/4 To 2 Cups All Purpose Flour
- 1/4 Cup Fine Cornmeal
- Toppings
- 1 Large Grilled Portobello Mushroom, Sliced
- 1 Jar Pickled Artichoke Hearts, Chopped
- 1 Cup Fontina Cheese, Shredded
- 1/2 Cup Shaved Parmigiano, Divided
- Chopped Roasted Garlic, To Taste
- 1/4 Cup Olive Oil
- Banana Peppers, To Taste
- Traeger Pizza Kit

Instructions:

- In a glass bowl, stir together the warm water, yeast, and sugar. Let stand until the mixture starts to foam, about 10 minutes.
- In a mixer, combine 1 3/4 cup flour, sugar, and salt. Stir oil into the yeast mixture. Slowly add the liquid to the dry ingredients while slowly increasing the mixers speed until fully combined. The dough should be smooth and not sticky.
- Knead the dough on a floured surface, gradually adding the remaining flour as needed to prevent the dough from sticking, until smooth, about 5-10 minutes. Form the dough into a ball.
- Apply a thin layer of olive oil to a large bowl. Place the dough into the bowl, and coat the dough ball with a small amount of olive oil. Cover and let rise in a warm place for about 1 hour, or until doubled in size.
- When ready to cook, set temperature to High and preheat, lid closed for 15 minutes.
- Place a pizza stone in the grill while it preheats.
- Punch the dough down and roll it out into a 12-inch circle on a floured surface.
- Spread the cornmeal evenly on the pizza peel. Place the dough on the pizza peel and assemble the toppings evenly in the following order: olive oil, roasted garlic, fontina, portobello, artichoke hearts, parmigiano and banana peppers.
- Carefully slide the assembled pizza from the pizza peel to the preheated pizza stone and bake until the crust is golden brown, about 10-12 minutes. Enjoy!

10.2 Braised Rabbit Stew
Ingredients:

- 1 (3 Lb.) Rabbit
- 2 Tbsp Butter
- 1 Medium Yellow Onion, Chopped
- 2 Cloves Garlic, Minced
- 1 Carrot, Peeled, Chopped
- 1 Stalk Celery, Chopped
- 2 Tbsp Flour
- 1 Sprig Thyme
- 2 Bay Leaves
- 1 Cup Red Wine
- 4 Cups Rabbit or Chicken Stock
- Salt and Pepper, To Taste

Instructions:

- Heat 1 tablespoon olive oil in Dutch oven over medium-high heat. When the oil is hot, brown the rabbit pieces in batches until golden brown and set aside.
- Add 2 tablespoons butter to the pan and when the butter is melted add the onion, carrot and celery. Saute 10 minutes until carrots are tender and onions are translucent. Add garlic and saute 1 minute more.
- Sprinkle flour over onion mixture, stir well, and cook for 1 minute more. While stirring, pour in red wine and chicken stock and place rabbit pieces back in making sure they're covered at least 3/4 of the way. Add bay leaves and thyme and bring liquid to a simmer.
- When ready to cook start the Traeger grill on smoke with the lid open until fire is established (4-5 minutes). Set the temperature to 300 degrees F and preheat, lid closed 10-15 minutes.
- Cover and transfer to the grill. Cook for 2 hours or until the rabbit is completely tender and pulls away from the bone. Top with some chopped parsley and serve with crusty bread. Enjoy!

10.3 Grilled Duck Breasts
Ingredients:

- 4 (6 Oz) Boneless Duck Breasts
- 1/4 Cup Traeger Big Game Rub

Instructions:

- Using a sharp knife, score the skin of the duck so it has a 1/4-inch diamond pattern.
- Season both sides of the duck with Traeger Big Game Rub.
- When ready to cook, set temperature to High and preheat, lid closed for 15 minutes.
- Place the duck breasts, skin side down, on the grate. Close the lid and cook for 15-20 minutes, or the internal temperature reaches 130-135°F (for medium rare) when an instant read thermometer is inserted into the thickest part of the breast.
- Remove from grill and allow to rest for 5 minutes. Slice against the grain and serve in thick slices. Enjoy!

10.4 Smoked Dry Rubbed Baby Back Ribs
Ingredients:

- 1/4 Cup Dark Brown Sugar
- 1/4 Cup Sea Salt
- 1/4 Cup Pimento (Spanish Smoked Paprika)
- 2 Tbsp Black Pepper
- 2 Tsp Granulated Onion
- 2 Tsp Granulated Garlic
- 1 Tsp Ground Cumin
- 1/2 Tsp Cinnamon
- 1/4 Tsp Ground Nutmeg
- Baby Back Ribs:
- 4 Racks (8 To 10 Lbs. Total) Baby Back Ribs
- 2 Cups Traeger Qu BBQ Sauce

Instructions:

- For the rub, combine all the rub ingredients in a small bowl and whisk to mix.
- If your butcher has not already done so, remove the thin silver skin from the bone-side of the ribs by working the tip of a butter knife or screwdriver underneath the membrane over a middle bone. Use paper towels to get a firm grip, then pull the membrane off.
- Sprinkle the rub over both sides of the ribs. Gently pat the seasonings onto the meat, but do not rub vigorously. You will need about 1-1/2 tablespoons of rub for each side.
- When ready to cook, start the Traeger grill on Smoke with the lid open until the fire is established (4 to 5 minutes). Set the temperature to 250 degrees F and preheat, lid closed, for 15 minutes.
- Place the ribs bone-side down on the grill grate. Smoke the ribs until browned, very tender, and the meat has shrunk back from the ends of the rib bones by 1/4-1/2 inch, about 3-1/2 to 4-1/2 hours.
- Remove the ribs from the grill grate and let rest. Increase the temperature of the Traeger to 375 degrees F and allow to preheat.
- Brush the ribs with Traeger Qu BBQ Sauce. Grill for 6 to 8 minutes per side, or until the sauce has set.
- Cut each rack into halves or individual ribs for serving. Enjoy

Chapter 11: Tricks, Tips, Tools & Cooking Time

11.1 Tools
Here are some accessories that I own and use to make my cooking experiences easier and more enjoyable.

- DIGITAL MEAT THERMOMETER—I cannot stress the importance of a good digital thermometer.
- SET OF KNIVES AND SCISSORS—Make sure you have a great set of sharp knives to use on raw and cooked meats.
- FLAME ZONE, OPEN FLAME TECHNOLOGY, DIRECT FLAME —Many wood pellet smoker-grill manufacturers now provide the technology for direct-flame grilling
- SEARING GRATES—There are different types of searing grates available depending on your unit.
- CHICKEN LEG/WING HANGER—Simply the best way to smoke/cook chicken legs and/or wings to perfection is with these hangers
- RIB RACK—A rib rack allows you to cook four to eight slabs of St. Louis– style, baby back, or spare ribs at one time
- TEFLON-COATED FIBERGLASS MATS—These indirect cooking mats keep food from sticking to grill grates and allow for easy cleanup
- BARBECUE INSULATED GLOVES—I use light, flexible insulated rubber gloves to protect my hands while handling and removing food directly from the grill, and pulling hot pork butts.
- MEAT SLICER—For precise meat slicing I use a 7-inch-blade meat slicer to eliminate the time-consuming process of slicing food by hand. For example, it works great to thinly slice tri-tip roasts for exquisite tri-tip sandwiches
- NONSTICK GRILLING TRAY—Great for grilling, roasting, or baking items like vegetables, fish, and small or delicate foods. Cleans easily with soap and water.
- PIZZA PADDLE—Your wood pellet smoker-grill cooks crispy, hot, delicious take-and-bake pizzas or made-from-scratch pies
- PIG TAIL FOOD FLIPPER—This tapered shaft has a sharp, spiral snare at the tip designed to lightly pierce the edge of any food to flip or move without trouble. Use it for steaks, chops, ribs, chicken, etc.

11.2 Cooking Tips & Tricks
Following are the cooking tips and tricks in wood pallet smoker grill.

11.2.1 Quality Meat and Seasonings
Don't overlook your friendly neighborhood butcher shop for great and custom cuts of meats, poultry, and sausages, as well as wonderful rubs, seasonings, and barbecue sauces.

11.2.2 FTC
A number of my recipes call for FTC resting the meat. This important acronym stands for "Foil–Towel–Cooler" and is a common method used for holding and/or resting cooked meats, such as pork butts, brisket, and turkey, in order to redistribute the juices into the meat. It produces a moist and tender finished product. Pitmasters, professionals, caterers, and restaurants use industrial units like a Cambro, for example, to achieve these results. FTC is lovingly referred to as the poor man's Cambro.

11.2.3 USDA Minimum Internal Temperatures
Cook all food to these minimum internal temperatures as measured with a digital food thermometer before removing from the heat source. You may choose to cook to higher temperatures for reasons of personal preference.

11.2.4 Indirect and Direct Grill Setup
All wood pellet smoker-grills are designed primarily for indirect cooking. Indirect cooking uses deflected heat to cook more slowly and evenly. As mentioned before, the heat deflector is a stainless-steel plate that sits above the firepot.

11.2.5 Recommended Wood Pellet Flavors
The wood pellets I recommend are just that, a recommendation. When you see multiple pellet recommendations my preferred pellet flavor for that recipe is always listed first. If you have another flavor profile you would like to accomplish, feel free to substitute it.

11.2.6 Prepping for The Grill
The prep section is all the work you do before bringing the food to the grill. The number one priority in the prep cycle is planning ahead. Give yourself plenty of time, read the recipe, and research any step or procedure you might have questions about.

11.2.7 Cooking Times
Cooking times in this book are given for planning purposes and can vary depending on what type of grill you have or what temperature your meat started at. Always determine the cooking time by the internal temperature reading of your food and not the cook time I have provided.

11.2.8 Preheating

Times for preheating your wood pellet smoker-grill may vary due to manufacturer-dependent startup procedures. The key is to run a few tests and know your grill.

11.2.9 Thawing Food

In order to be safe and prevent illness, always thaw food in the refrigerator; submerge it in cold water, changing the water every 30 minutes making sure the food stays submerged; or use the defrost setting in a microwave. Do not thaw your frozen food on the countertop.

11.2.10 Internal Temperature

Always cook to internal temperatures preferably using a digital instant-read thermometer like a Thermapen or equivalent unit. Probe thermometers should be inserted before placing the protein on the grill and should be placed in the thickest part of the meat, not touching the bone.

CPSIA information can be obtained
at www.ICGtesting.com
Printed in the USA
LVHW100954211120
672149LV00008B/238